www.EffortlessMath.com

... So Much More Online!

✓ FREE Math lessons

✓ More Math learning books!

✓ Mathematics Worksheets

✓ Online Math Tutors

Need a PDF version of this book?

Send email to: Info@EffortlessMath.com

D1295538

Ace the ATI TEAS 6 Math in 30 Days

The Ultimate Crash Course to Beat the ATI TEAS 6 Math Test

By

Reza Nazari

& Ava Ross

ISBN–13: 978-1-970036-80-0

ISBN–10: 1-970036-80-X

Published by: Effortless Math Education Inc.

www.EffortlessMath.com

Welcome to
ATI TEAS 6 Math Prep
2021

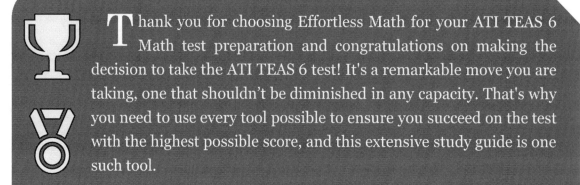

Thank you for choosing Effortless Math for your ATI TEAS 6 Math test preparation and congratulations on making the decision to take the ATI TEAS 6 test! It's a remarkable move you are taking, one that shouldn't be diminished in any capacity. That's why you need to use every tool possible to ensure you succeed on the test with the highest possible score, and this extensive study guide is one such tool.

If math has never been a strong subject for you, don't worry! This book will help you prepare for (and even ACE) the ATI TEAS 6 test's math section. As test day draws nearer, effective preparation becomes increasingly more important. Thankfully, you have this comprehensive study guide to help you get ready for the test. With this guide, you can feel confident that you will be more than ready for the TEAS 6 Math test when the time comes.

First and foremost, it is important to note that this book is a study guide and not a textbook. It is best read from cover to cover. Every lesson of this "self-guided math book" was carefully developed to ensure that you are making the most effective use of your time while preparing for the test. This up-to-date guide reflects the 2021 test guidelines and will put you on the right track to hone your math skills, overcome exam anxiety, and boost your confidence, so that you can have your best to succeed on the TEAS 6 Math test.

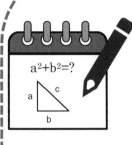

This study guide will:

☑ Explain the format of the ATI TEAS 6 Math test.

☑ Describe specific test-taking strategies that you can use on the test.

☑ Provide TEAS 6 Math test-taking tips.

☑ Review all TEAS 6 Math concepts and topics you will be tested on.

☑ Help you identify the areas in which you need to concentrate your study time.

☑ Offer exercises that help you develop the basic math skills you will learn in each section.

☑ Give **2 realistic and full-length practice tests** (featuring new question types) with detailed answers to help you measure your exam readiness and build confidence.

This resource contains everything you will ever need to succeed on the TEAS 6 Math test. You'll get in-depth instructions on every math topic as well as tips and techniques on how to answer each question type. You'll also get plenty of practice questions to boost your test-taking confidence.

In addition, in the following pages you'll find:

➢ **How to Use This Book Effectively** – This section provides you with step-by-step instructions on how to get the most out of this comprehensive study guide.

➢ **How to study for the ATI TEAS 6 Math Test** – A six-step study program has been developed to help you make the best use of this book and prepare for your TEAS 6 Math test. Here you'll find tips and strategies to guide your study program and help you understand TEAS 6 Math and how to ace the test.

➢ **ATI TEAS 6 Math Review** – Learn everything you need to know about the TEAS 6 Math test.

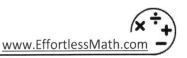

➢ **ATI TEAS 6 Math Test-Taking Strategies** – Learn how to effectively put these recommended test-taking techniques into use for improving your TEAS 6 Math score.

➢ **Test Day Tips** – Review these tips to make sure you will do your best when the big day comes.

Effortless Math's ATI TEAS 6 Online Center

Effortless Math Online ATI TEAS 6 Center offers a complete study program, including the following:

✓ Step-by-step instructions on how to prepare for the TEAS 6 Math test

✓ Numerous TEAS 6 Math worksheets to help you measure your math skills

✓ Complete list of ATI TEAS 6 Math formulas

✓ Video lessons for all ATI TEAS 6 Math topics

✓ Full-length ATI TEAS 6 Math practice tests

✓ And much more…

No Registration Required.

Visit **EffortlessMath.com/ATITEAS6** to find your online ATI TEAS 6 Math resources.

How to Use This Book Effectively

Look no further when you need a study guide to improve your math skills to succeed on the math portion of the ATI TEAS 6 test. Each chapter of this comprehensive guide to the ATI TEAS 6 Math will provide you with the knowledge, tools, and understanding needed for every topic covered on the test.

It's imperative that you understand each topic before moving onto another one, as that's the way to guarantee your success. Each chapter provides you with examples and a step-by-step guide of every concept to better understand the content that will be on the test. To get the best possible results from this book:

➢ **Begin studying long before your test date.** This provides you ample time to learn the different math concepts. The earlier you begin studying for the test, the sharper your skills will be. Do not procrastinate! Provide yourself with plenty of time (at least 30 days) to learn the concepts and feel comfortable that you understand them when your test date arrives.

➢ **Practice consistently.** Study TEAS 6 Math concepts at least 20 to 30 minutes a day. Remember, slow and steady wins the race, which can be applied to preparing for the TEAS 6 Math test. Instead of cramming to tackle everything at once, be patient and learn the math topics in short bursts.

➢ Whenever you get a math problem wrong, **mark it off, and review it later** to make sure you understand the concept.

➢ Start each session by **looking over the previous material.**

➢ Once you've reviewed the book's lessons, **take the practice tests** on Day 29 to gauge your level of readiness. Then, review your results. Read detailed answers and solutions for each question you missed.

➢ **Take another practice test** (on Day 30) to get an idea of how ready you are to take the actual exam. Taking the practice tests will give you the confidence you need on test day. Simulate the ATI TEAS 6 testing environment by sitting in a quiet room free from distraction. Make sure to clock yourself with a timer.

How to Study for the ATI TEAS 6 Math Test

Studying for the ATI TEAS 6 Math test can be a really daunting and boring task. What's the best way to go about it? Is there a certain study method that works better than others? Well, studying for the ATI TEAS 6 Math can be done effectively. The following six-step program has been designed to make preparing for the TEAS 6 Math test more efficient and less overwhelming.

Step **1** - Create a study plan
Step **2** - Choose your study resources
Step **3** - Review, Learn, Practice
Step **4** - Learn and practice test-taking strategies
Step **5** - Learn the ATI TEAS 6 Test format and take practice tests
Step **6** - Analyze your performance

STEP 1: Create a Study Plan

It's always easier to get things done when you have a plan. Creating a study plan for the ATI TEAS 6 Math test can help you to stay on track with your studies. It's important to sit down and prepare a study plan with what works with your life, work, and any other obligations you may have. Devote enough time each day to studying. It's also a great idea to break down each section of the exam into blocks and study one concept at a time.

It's important to understand that there is no "right" way to create a study plan. Your study plan will be personalized based on your specific needs and learning style.

Follow these guidelines to create an effective study plan for your ATI TEAS 6 Math test:

★ **Analyze your learning style and study habits** – Everyone has a different learning style. It is essential to embrace your individuality and the unique way you learn. Think about what works and what doesn't work for you. Do you prefer ATI TEAS 6 Math prep books or a combination of textbooks and video lessons? Does it work better for you if you study every night for thirty minutes or is it more effective to study in the morning before going to work?

★ **Evaluate your schedule** – Review your current schedule and find out how much time you can consistently devote to ATI TEAS 6 Math study.

★ **Develop a schedule** – Now it's time to add your study schedule to your calendar like any other obligation. Schedule time for study, practice, and review. Plan out which topic you will study on which day to ensure that you're devoting enough time to each concept. Develop a study plan that is mindful, realistic, and flexible.

★ **Stick to your schedule** – A study plan is only effective when it is followed consistently. You should try to develop a study plan that you can follow for the length of your study program.

★ **Evaluate your study plan and adjust as needed** – Sometimes you need to adjust your plan when you have new commitments. Check in with yourself regularly to make sure that you're not falling behind in your study plan. Remember, the most important thing is sticking to your plan. Your study plan is all about helping you be more productive. If you find that your study plan is not as effective as you want, don't get discouraged. It's okay to make changes as you figure out what works best for you.

STEP 2: Choose Your Study Resources

There are numerous textbooks and online resources available for the ATI TEAS 6 Math test, and it may not be clear where to begin. Don't worry! This study guide provides everything you need to fully prepare for your ATI TEAS 6 Math test. In addition to the book content, you can also use Effortless Math's online resources. (video lessons, worksheets, formulas, etc.)

Simply visit EffortlessMath.com/ATITEAS6 to find your online ATI TEAS 6 Math resources.

STEP 3: Review, Learn, Practice

This ATI TEAS 6 Math study guide breaks down each subject into specific skills or content areas. For instance, the percent concept is separated into different topics–percent calculation, percent increase and decrease, percent problems, etc. Use this book to help you go over all key math concepts and topics on the ATI TEAS 6 Math test.

As you read each chapter, take notes or highlight the concepts you would like to go over again in the future. If you're unfamiliar with a topic or something is difficult for you, do additional research on it. For each math topic, plenty of instructions, step-by-step guides, and examples are provided to ensure you get a good grasp of the material. You can also find video lessons on the Effortless Math website for each ATI TEAS 6 Math concept.

Quickly review the topics you do understand to get a brush-up of the material. Be sure to do the practice questions provided at the end of every chapter to measure your understanding of the concepts.

STEP 4: Learn and Practice Test-taking Strategies

In the following sections, you will find important test-taking strategies and tips that can help you earn extra points. You'll learn how to think strategically and when to guess if you don't know the answer to a question. Using ATI TEAS 6 Math test-taking strategies and tips can help you raise your score and do well on the test. Apply test taking strategies on the practice tests to help you boost your confidence.

STEP 5: Learn the ATI TEAS 6 Test Format and Take Practice Tests

The *ATI TEAS 6 Test Review* section provides information about the structure of the TEAS 6 test. Read this section to learn more about the TEAS 6 test structure, different test sections, the number of questions in each section, and the section time limits. When you have a prior understanding of the test format and different types of TEAS 6 Math questions, you'll feel more confident when you take the actual exam.

Once you have read through the instructions and lessons and feel like you are ready to go – take advantage of both of the full-length TEAS 6 Math practice tests available in this study guide on Days 29 and 30. Use the practice tests to sharpen your skills and build confidence.

The ATI TEAS 6 Math practice tests offered at the end of the book are formatted similarly to the actual TEAS 6 Math test. When you take each practice test, try to simulate actual testing conditions. To take the practice tests, sit in a quiet space, time yourself, and work through as many of the questions as time allows. The practice tests are followed by detailed answer explanations to help you find your weak areas, learn from your mistakes, and raise your ATI TEAS 6 Math score.

STEP 6: Analyze Your Performance

After taking the practice tests, look over the answer keys and explanations to learn which questions you answered correctly and which you did not. Never be discouraged if you make a few mistakes. See them as a learning opportunity. This will highlight your strengths and weaknesses.

You can use the results to determine if you need additional practice or if you are ready to take the actual ATI TEAS 6 Math test.

Looking for more?

Visit <u>EffortlessMath.com/ATITEAS6</u> to find hundreds of ATI TEAS 6 Math worksheets, video tutorials, practice tests, ATI TEAS 6 Math formulas, and much more.

Or scan this QR code.

No Registration Required.

ATI TEAS 6 Test Review

The ATI TEAS (Test of Essential Academic Skills), known as TEAS, is an admissions test for nursing schools, and is designed to assess a student's preparedness entering the health science fields. The last edition (the sixth edition) of the test, called the ATI TEAS 6 Test, was published by ATI Testing on August 31, 2016.

The ATI TEAS 6 Test consists of four multiple-choice sections:

- ✓ **Reading:** 53 Questions – 64 Minutes
- ✓ **Mathematics:** 36 Questions – 54 Minutes
- ✓ **Science:** 53 Questions – 63 Minutes
- ✓ **English and Language Usage:** 28 Questions – 28 Minutes

The Math portion will consist of around 36 multiple-choice questions. It covers two main topics: Number and Algebra; Measurement and Data.

Test takers will be allowed to use a four-function calculator during the Math section of the ATI TEAS 6 test. A calculator will be included in the online version and students will be issued one at the testing center during a paper and pencil test.

ATI TEAS 6 Math Test-Taking Strategies

Here are some test-taking strategies that you can use to maximize your performance and results on the ATI TEAS 6 Math test.

#1 : USE THIS APPROACH TO ANSWER EVERY ATI TEAS 6 MATH QUESTION

- Review the question to identify keywords and important information.

- Translate the keywords into math operations so you can solve the problem.

- Review the answer choices. What are the differences between answer choices?

- Draw or label a diagram if needed.

- Try to find patterns.

- Find the right method to answer the question. Use straightforward math, plug in numbers, or test the answer choices (backsolving).

- Double-check your work.

#2 : USE EDUCATED GUESSING

This approach is applicable to the problems you understand to some degree but cannot solve using straightforward math. In such cases, try to filter out as many answer choices as possible before picking an answer. In cases where you don't have a clue about what a certain problem entails, don't waste any time trying to eliminate answer choices. Just choose one randomly before moving onto the next question.

As you can ascertain, direct solutions are the most optimal approach. Carefully read through the question, determine what the solution is using the math you have learned before, then coordinate the answer with one of the choices available to you. Are you stumped? Make your best guess, then move on.

Don't leave any fields empty! Even if you're unable to work out a problem, strive to answer it. Take a guess if you have to. You will not lose points by getting an answer wrong, though you may gain a point by getting it correct!

#3 : BALLPARK

A ballpark answer is a rough approximation. When we become overwhelmed by calculations and figures, we end up making silly mistakes. A decimal that is moved by one unit can change an answer from right to wrong, regardless of the number of steps that you went through to get it. That's where ballparking can play a big part.

If you think you know what the correct answer may be (even if it's just a ballpark answer), you'll usually have the ability to eliminate a couple of choices. While answer choices are usually based on the average student error and/or values that are closely tied, you will still be able to weed out choices that are way far afield. Try to find answers that aren't in the proverbial ballpark when you're looking for a wrong answer on a multiple-choice question. This is an optimal approach to eliminating answers to a problem.

#4 : BACKSOLVING

All questions on the ATI TEAS 6 Math test will be in multiple-choice format. Many test-takers prefer multiple-choice questions, as at least the answer is right there. You'll typically have four answers to pick from. You simply need to figure out which one is correct. Usually, the best way to go about doing so is "backsolving."

As mentioned earlier, direct solutions are the most optimal approach to answering a question. Carefully read through a problem, calculate a solution, then correspond the answer with one of the choices displayed in front of you. If you can't calculate a solution, your next best approach involves "backsolving."

When backsolving a problem, contrast one of your answer options against the problem you are asked, then see which of them is most relevant. More often than not, answer choices are listed in ascending or descending order. In such cases, try out the choices B or C. If it's not correct, you can go either down or up from there.

#5 : Plugging In Numbers

"Plugging in numbers" is a strategy that can be applied to a wide range of different math problems on the ATI TEAS 6 Math test. This approach is typically used to simplify a challenging question so that it is more understandable. By using the strategy carefully, you can find the answer without too much trouble.

The concept is fairly straightforward–replace unknown variables in a problem with certain values. When selecting a number, consider the following:

- Choose a number that's basic (just not too basic). Generally, you should avoid choosing 1 (or even 0). A decent choice is 2.

- Try not to choose a number that is displayed in the problem.

- Make sure you keep your numbers different if you need to choose at least two of them.

- More often than not, choosing numbers merely lets you filter out some of your answer choices. As such, don't just go with the first choice that gives you the right answer.

- If several answers seem correct, then you'll need to choose another value and try again. This time, though, you'll just need to check choices that haven't been eliminated yet.

- If your question contains fractions, then a potential right answer may involve either an LCD (least common denominator) or an LCD multiple.

- 100 is the number you should choose when you are dealing with problems involving percentages.

ATI TEAS 6 Mathematics Test – Daytime Tips

After practicing and reviewing all the math concepts you've been taught, and taking some ATI TEAS 6 mathematics practice tests, you'll be prepared for test day. Consider the following tips to be extra-ready come test time.

Before Your Test

What to do the night before:

- **Relax!** One day before your test, study lightly or skip studying altogether. You shouldn't attempt to learn something new, either. There are plenty of reasons why studying the evening before a big test can work against you. Put it this way–a marathoner wouldn't go out for a sprint before the day of a big race. Mental marathoners–such as yourself–should not study for any more than one hour 24 hours before a ATI TEAS 6 test. That's because your brain requires some rest to be at its best. The night before your exam, spend some time with family or friends, or read a book.

- **Avoid bright screens** - You'll have to get some good shuteye the night before your test. Bright screens (such as the ones coming from your laptop, TV, or mobile device) should be avoided altogether. Staring at such a screen will keep your brain up, making it hard to drift asleep at a reasonable hour.

- **Make sure your dinner is healthy** - The meal that you have for dinner should be nutritious. Be sure to drink plenty of water as well. Load up on your complex carbohydrates, much like a marathon runner would do. Pasta, rice, and potatoes are ideal options here, as are vegetables and protein sources.

- **Get your bag ready for test day** - The night prior to your test, pack your bag with your stationery, admissions pass, ID, and any other gear that you need. Keep the bag right by your front door.

- **Make plans to reach the testing site** - Before going to sleep, ensure that you understand precisely how you will arrive at the site of the test. If parking is something you'll have to find first, plan for it. If you're dependent on public transit, then review the schedule. You should also make sure that the

train/bus/subway/streetcar you use will be running. Find out about road closures as well. If a parent or friend is accompanying you, ensure that they understand what steps they have to take as well.

The Day of the Test

- **Get up reasonably early, but not too early.**

- **Have breakfast** - Breakfast improves your concentration, memory, and mood. As such, make sure the breakfast that you eat in the morning is healthy. The last thing you want to be is distracted by a grumbling tummy. If it's not your own stomach making those noises, another test taker close to you might be instead. Prevent discomfort or embarrassment by consuming a healthy breakfast. Bring a snack with you if you think you'll need it.

- **Follow your daily routine** - Do you watch Good Morning America each morning while getting ready for the day? Don't break your usual habits on the day of the test. Likewise, if coffee isn't something you drink in the morning, then don't take up the habit hours before your test. Routine consistency lets you concentrate on the main objective–doing the best you can on your test.

- **Wear layers** - Dress yourself up in comfortable layers. You should be ready for any kind of internal temperature. If it gets too warm during the test, take a layer off.

- **Get there on time** - The last thing you want to do is get to the test site late. Rather, you should be there 45 minutes prior to the start of the test. Upon your arrival, try not to hang out with anybody who is nervous. Any anxious energy they exhibit shouldn't influence you.

- **Leave the books at home** - No books should be brought to the test site. If you start developing anxiety before the test, books could encourage you to do some last-minute studying, which will only hinder you. Keep the books far away–better yet, leave them at home.

- **Make your voice heard** - If something is off, speak to a proctor. If medical attention is needed or if you'll require anything, consult the proctor prior to the start of the test. Any doubts you have should be clarified. You should be entering the test site with a state of mind that is completely clear.

- **Have faith in yourself** - When you feel confident, you will be able to perform at your best. When you are waiting for the test to begin, envision yourself receiving an outstanding result. Try to see yourself as someone who knows all the answers, no matter what the questions are. A lot of athletes tend to use this technique–particularly before a big competition. Your expectations will be reflected by your performance.

During your test

- **Be calm and breathe deeply** - You need to relax before the test, and some deep breathing will go a long way to help you do that. Be confident and calm. You got this. Everybody feels a little stressed out just before an evaluation of any kind is set to begin. Learn some effective breathing exercises. Spend a minute meditating before the test starts. Filter out any negative thoughts you have. Exhibit confidence when having such thoughts.

- **Concentrate on the test** - Refrain from comparing yourself to anyone else. You shouldn't be distracted by the people near you or random noise. Concentrate exclusively on the test. If you find yourself irritated by surrounding noises, earplugs can be used to block sounds off close to you. Don't forget–the test is going to last several hours if you're taking more than one subject of the test. Some of that time will be dedicated to brief sections. Concentrate on the specific section you are working on during a particular moment. Do not let your mind wander off to upcoming or previous sections.

- **Try to answer each question individually** - Focus only on the question you are working on. Use one of the test-taking strategies to solve the problem. If you aren't able to come up with an answer, don't get frustrated. Simply skip that question, then move onto the next one.

- **Don't forget to breathe!** Whenever you notice your mind wandering, your stress levels boosting, or frustration brewing, take a thirty-second break. Shut your eyes, drop your pencil, breathe deeply, and let your shoulders relax. You will end up being more productive when you allow yourself to relax for a moment.

- **Optimize your breaks** - When break time comes, use the restroom, have a snack, and reactivate your energy for the subsequent section. Doing some stretches can help stimulate your blood flow.

After your test

- **Take it easy** - You will need to set some time aside to relax and decompress once the test has concluded. There is no need to stress yourself out about what you could've said, or what you may have done wrong. At this point, there's nothing you can do about it. Your energy and time would be better spent on something that will bring you happiness for the remainder of your day.

- **Redoing the test** - Did you pass the test? Congratulations! Your hard work paid off!

  If you have failed your test, though, don't worry! The test can be retaken. In such cases, you will need to follow the retake policy. You also need to re-register to take the exam again.

Contents

Day 1: Fractions

Math Topics that you'll learn today:

- ✓ Simplifying Fractions

- ✓ Adding and Subtracting Fractions

- ✓ Multiplying and Dividing Fractions

"A Man is like a fraction whose numerator is what he is and whose denominator is what he thinks of himself. The larger the denominator, the smaller the fraction." ~Tolstoy

Simplifying Fractions

Step-by-step guide:

✓ Evenly divide both the top and bottom of the fraction by $2, 3, 5, 7, \ldots$ etc.

✓ Continue until you can't go any further.

Examples:

1) Simplify $\frac{12}{20}$.

To simplify $\frac{12}{20}$, find a number that both 12 and 20 are divisible by. Both are divisible by 4.

Then: $\frac{12}{20} = \frac{12 \div 4}{20 \div 4} = \frac{3}{5}$

2) Simplify $\frac{64}{80}$.

To simplify $\frac{64}{80}$, find a number that both 64 and 80 are divisible by. Both are divisible by 8 and 16. Then: $\frac{64}{80} = \frac{64 \div 8}{80 \div 8} = \frac{8}{10}$, 8 and 10 are divisible by 2, then: $\frac{8}{10} = \frac{4}{5}$

or $\frac{64}{80} = \frac{64 \div 16}{80 \div 16} = \frac{4}{5}$

✎ *Simplify each fraction.*

1) $\dfrac{9}{18} =$ 5) $\dfrac{18}{24} =$ 9) $\dfrac{18}{36} =$

2) $\dfrac{8}{10} =$ 6) $\dfrac{6}{9} =$ 10) $\dfrac{6}{42} =$

3) $\dfrac{6}{8} =$ 7) $\dfrac{12}{15} =$ 11) $\dfrac{13}{39} =$

4) $\dfrac{5}{20} =$ 8) $\dfrac{4}{16} =$ 12) $\dfrac{21}{28} =$

Adding and Subtracting Fractions

Step-by-step guide:

- ✓ For "like" fractions (fractions with the same denominator), add or subtract the numerators and write the answer over the common denominator.
- ✓ Find equivalent fractions with the same denominator before you can add or subtract fractions with different denominators.
- ✓ Adding and Subtracting with the same denominator:

$$\frac{a}{b} + \frac{c}{b} = \frac{a+c}{b} \ , \ \frac{a}{b} - \frac{c}{b} = \frac{a-c}{b}$$

- ✓ Adding and Subtracting fractions with different denominators:

$$\frac{a}{b} + \frac{c}{d} = \frac{ad+c}{bd} \ , \ \frac{a}{b} - \frac{c}{d} = \frac{ad-cb}{bd}$$

Examples:

1) Subtract fractions. $\frac{4}{5} - \frac{3}{5} =$

For "like" fractions, subtract the numerators and write the answer over the common denominator. then: $\frac{4}{5} - \frac{3}{5} = \frac{1}{5}$

2) Subtract fractions. $\frac{2}{3} - \frac{1}{2} =$

For "unlike" fractions, find equivalent fractions with the same denominator before you can add or subtract fractions with different denominators. Use this formula: $\frac{a}{b} - \frac{c}{d} = \frac{ad-cb}{bd}$

$$\frac{2}{3} - \frac{1}{2} = \frac{(2)(2) - (1)(3)}{3 \times 2} = \frac{4-3}{6} = \frac{1}{6}$$

🖎 *Find the sum or difference.*

1) $\frac{1}{3} + \frac{2}{3} =$

2) $\frac{1}{2} + \frac{1}{3} =$

3) $\frac{2}{5} + \frac{1}{2} =$

4) $\frac{3}{7} + \frac{2}{3} =$

5) $\frac{1}{2} - \frac{1}{3} =$

6) $\frac{4}{5} - \frac{2}{3} =$

7) $\frac{2}{3} - \frac{1}{6} =$

8) $\frac{3}{5} - \frac{1}{2} =$

9) $\frac{8}{9} - \frac{2}{5} =$

Multiplying and Dividing Fractions

Step-by-step guide:

- ✓ Multiplying fractions: multiply the top numbers and multiply the bottom numbers.
- ✓ Dividing fractions: Keep, Change, Flip
- ✓ Keep first fraction, change division sign to multiplication, and flip the numerator and denominator of the second fraction. Then, solve!

Examples:

1) Multiplying fractions. $\frac{5}{6} \times \frac{3}{4} =$

Multiply the top numbers and multiply the bottom numbers.

$\frac{5}{6} \times \frac{3}{4} = \frac{5 \times 3}{6 \times 4} = \frac{15}{24}$, simplify: $\frac{15}{24} = \frac{15 \div 3}{24 \div 3} = \frac{5}{8}$

2) Dividing fractions. $\frac{1}{4} \div \frac{2}{3} =$

Keep first fraction, change division sign to multiplication, and flip the numerator and denominator of the second fraction. Then: $\frac{1}{4} \times \frac{3}{2} = \frac{1 \times 3}{4 \times 2} = \frac{3}{8}$

✒ Find the answers.

1) $\frac{1}{2} \times \frac{3}{4} =$

2) $\frac{3}{5} \times \frac{2}{3} =$

3) $\frac{1}{4} \times \frac{2}{5} =$

4) $\frac{1}{6} \times \frac{4}{5} =$

5) $\frac{1}{5} \times \frac{1}{4} =$

6) $\frac{2}{5} \times \frac{1}{2} =$

7) $\frac{1}{2} \div \frac{1}{4} =$

8) $\frac{1}{3} \div \frac{1}{2} =$

9) $\frac{2}{5} \div \frac{1}{3} =$

10) $\frac{1}{4} \div \frac{2}{3} =$

11) $\frac{1}{5} \div \frac{3}{10} =$

12) $\frac{2}{7} \div \frac{1}{3} =$

Answers – Day 1

Simplifying Fractions

1) $\dfrac{1}{2}$ 5) $\dfrac{3}{4}$ 9) $\dfrac{1}{2}$

2) $\dfrac{4}{5}$ 6) $\dfrac{2}{3}$ 10) $\dfrac{1}{7}$

3) $\dfrac{3}{4}$ 7) $\dfrac{4}{5}$ 11) $\dfrac{1}{3}$

4) $\dfrac{1}{4}$ 8) $\dfrac{1}{4}$ 12) $\dfrac{3}{4}$

Adding and Subtracting Fractions

1) $\dfrac{3}{3} = 1$ 4) $\dfrac{23}{21}$ 7) $\dfrac{1}{2}$

2) $\dfrac{5}{6}$ 5) $\dfrac{1}{6}$ 8) $\dfrac{1}{10}$

3) $\dfrac{9}{10}$ 6) $\dfrac{2}{15}$ 9) $\dfrac{22}{45}$

Multiplying and Dividing Fractions

1) $\dfrac{3}{8}$ 5) $\dfrac{1}{20}$ 9) $\dfrac{6}{5}$

2) $\dfrac{2}{5}$ 6) $\dfrac{1}{5}$ 10) $\dfrac{3}{8}$

3) $\dfrac{1}{10}$ 7) 2 11) $\dfrac{2}{3}$

4) $\dfrac{2}{15}$ 8) $\dfrac{2}{3}$ 12) $\dfrac{6}{7}$

Day 2: Adding and Subtracting Mixed Numbers

Math Topics that you'll learn today:

- ✓ Adding Mixed Numbers

- ✓ Subtracting Mixed Numbers

"Wherever there is number, there is beauty." ~Proclus

Adding Mixed Numbers

Step-by-step guide:

Use the following steps for both adding and subtracting mixed numbers.

- ✓ Add whole numbers of the mixed numbers.
- ✓ Add the fractions of each mixed number.
- ✓ Find the Least Common Denominator (LCD) if necessary.
- ✓ Add whole numbers and fractions.
- ✓ Write your answer in lowest terms.

Examples:

1) Add mixed numbers. $1\frac{3}{4} + 2\frac{3}{8} =$

Rewriting our equation with parts separated, $1 + \frac{3}{4} + 2 + \frac{3}{8}$, Solving the whole number parts $1 + 2 = 3$, Solving the fraction parts $\frac{3}{4} + \frac{3}{8}$, and rewrite to solve with the equivalent fractions.

$\frac{6}{8} + \frac{3}{8} = \frac{9}{8} = 1\frac{1}{8}$, then Combining the whole and fraction parts $3 + 1 + \frac{1}{8} = 4\frac{1}{8}$

2) Add mixed numbers. $1\frac{2}{3} + 4\frac{1}{6} =$

Rewriting our equation with parts separated, $1 + \frac{2}{3} + 4 + \frac{1}{6}$, Solving the whole number parts $1 + 4 = 5$, Solving the fraction parts $\frac{2}{3} + \frac{1}{6}$, and rewrite to solve with the equivalent fractions.

$\frac{4}{6} + \frac{1}{6} = \frac{5}{6}$, then Combining the whole and fraction parts $5 + \frac{5}{6} = 5\frac{5}{6}$

✎ Find the sum.

1) $2\frac{1}{2} + 1\frac{1}{3} =$

2) $6\frac{1}{2} + 3\frac{1}{2} =$

3) $2\frac{3}{8} + 3\frac{1}{8} =$

4) $4\frac{1}{2} + 1\frac{1}{4} =$

5) $1\frac{3}{7} + 1\frac{5}{14} =$

6) $6\frac{5}{12} + 3\frac{3}{4} =$

7) $5\frac{1}{2} + 8\frac{3}{4} =$

8) $3\frac{7}{8} + 3\frac{1}{3} =$

9) $3\frac{3}{9} + 7\frac{6}{11} =$

Subtracting Mixed Numbers

Step-by-step guide:

Use the following steps for both adding and subtracting mixed numbers.

✓ Subtract the whole number of second mixed number from whole number of the first mixed number.
✓ Subtract the second fraction from the first one.
✓ Find the Least Common Denominator (LCD) if necessary.
✓ Add the result of whole numbers and fractions.
✓ Write your answer in lowest terms.

Examples:

1) Subtract. $5\frac{2}{3} - 2\frac{1}{4} =$

Rewriting our equation with parts separated, $5 + \frac{2}{3} - 2 - \frac{1}{4}$

Solving the whole number parts $5 - 2 = 3$, Solving the fraction parts, $\frac{2}{3} - \frac{1}{4} = \frac{8-3}{12} = \frac{5}{12}$

Combining the whole and fraction parts, $3 + \frac{5}{12} = 3\frac{5}{12}$

2) Subtract. $3\frac{4}{5} - 1\frac{1}{2} =$

Rewriting our equation with parts separated, $3 + \frac{4}{5} - 1 - \frac{1}{2}$

Solving the whole number parts $3 - 1 = 2$, Solving the fraction parts, $\frac{4}{5} - \frac{1}{2} = \frac{8-5}{10} = \frac{3}{10}$

Combining the whole and fraction parts, $2 + \frac{3}{10} = 2\frac{3}{10}$

✍ *Find the difference.*

1) $3\frac{1}{3} - 1\frac{1}{3} =$

2) $4\frac{1}{2} - 3\frac{1}{2} =$

3) $5\frac{1}{2} - 2\frac{1}{4} =$

4) $6\frac{1}{6} - 5\frac{1}{3} =$

5) $8\frac{1}{2} - 1\frac{1}{10} =$

6) $9\frac{1}{2} - 2\frac{1}{4} =$

7) $9\frac{1}{5} - 5\frac{1}{6} =$

8) $14\frac{3}{10} - 13\frac{1}{3} =$

9) $19\frac{2}{3} - 11\frac{5}{8} =$

Answers – Day 2

Adding Mixed Numbers

1) $3\frac{5}{6}$

2) 10

3) $5\frac{1}{2}$

4) $5\frac{3}{4}$

5) $2\frac{11}{14}$

6) $10\frac{1}{6}$

7) $14\frac{1}{4}$

8) $7\frac{5}{24}$

9) $10\frac{29}{33}$

Subtract Mixed Numbers

1) 2

2) 1

3) $3\frac{1}{4}$

4) $\frac{5}{6}$

5) $7\frac{2}{5}$

6) $7\frac{1}{4}$

7) $4\frac{1}{30}$

8) $\frac{29}{30}$

9) $8\frac{1}{24}$

Day 3: Multiplying and Dividing Mixed Numbers

Math Topics that you'll learn today:

✓ Multiplying Mixed Numbers

✓ Dividing Mixed Numbers

Mathematics is no more computation than typing is literature.

– John Allen Paulos

Multiplying Mixed Numbers

Step-by-step guide:

- ✓ Convert the mixed numbers to improper fractions. (improper fraction is a fraction in which the top number is bigger than bottom number)
- ✓ Multiply fractions and simplify if necessary.

$$a\frac{c}{b} = a + \frac{c}{b} = \frac{ab + c}{b}$$

Examples:

1) Multiply mixed numbers. $3\frac{2}{3} \times 2\frac{1}{2} =$

   Converting mixed numbers to fractions, $3\frac{2}{3} = \frac{11}{3}$ and $2\frac{1}{2} = \frac{5}{2}$.

   $\frac{11}{3} \times \frac{5}{2}$, Applying the fractions formula for multiplication, $\frac{11 \times 5}{3 \times 2} = \frac{55}{6} = 9\frac{1}{6}$

2) Solve. $4\frac{3}{5} \times 2\frac{1}{3} =$

   Converting mixed numbers to fractions, $\frac{23}{5} \times \frac{7}{3}$, Applying the fractions formula for multiplication, $\frac{23 \times 7}{5 \times 3} = \frac{161}{15} = 10\frac{11}{15}$

✎ *Find the product.*

1) $4\frac{1}{3} \times 2\frac{1}{5} =$

2) $3\frac{1}{2} \times 3\frac{1}{4} =$

3) $5\frac{2}{5} \times 2\frac{1}{3} =$

4) $2\frac{1}{2} \times 1\frac{2}{9} =$

5) $3\frac{4}{7} \times 2\frac{3}{5} =$

6) $7\frac{2}{3} \times 2\frac{2}{3} =$

7) $9\frac{8}{9} \times 8\frac{3}{4} =$

8) $2\frac{4}{7} \times 5\frac{2}{9} =$

9) $5\frac{2}{5} \times 2\frac{3}{5} =$

10) $3\frac{5}{7} \times 3\frac{5}{6} =$

Dividing Mixed Numbers

Step-by-step guide:

✓ Convert the mixed numbers to improper fractions.

✓ Divide fractions and simplify if necessary.

$$a\frac{c}{b} = a + \frac{c}{b} = \frac{ab+c}{b}$$

Examples:

1) Find the quotient. $2\frac{1}{2} \div 1\frac{1}{5} =$

Converting mixed numbers to fractions, $\frac{5}{2} \div \frac{6}{5}$, Applying the fractions formula for multiplication, $\frac{5\times5}{2\times6} = \frac{25}{12} = 2\frac{1}{12}$

2) Find the quotient. $4\frac{3}{4} \div 3\frac{4}{5} =$

Converting mixed numbers to fractions, $\frac{19}{4} \div \frac{19}{5}$, Applying the fractions formula for multiplication, $\frac{19\times5}{4\times19} = \frac{95}{76} = 1\frac{1}{4}$

✎ *Find the quotient.*

1) $1\frac{2}{3} \div 3\frac{1}{3} =$

2) $2\frac{1}{4} \div 1\frac{1}{2} =$

3) $10\frac{1}{2} \div 1\frac{2}{3} =$

4) $3\frac{1}{6} \div 4\frac{2}{3} =$

5) $4\frac{1}{8} \div 2\frac{1}{2} =$

6) $2\frac{1}{10} \div 2\frac{3}{5} =$

7) $1\frac{4}{11} \div 1\frac{1}{4} =$

8) $9\frac{1}{2} \div 9\frac{2}{3} =$

9) $8\frac{3}{4} \div 2\frac{2}{5} =$

10) $12\frac{1}{2} \div 9\frac{1}{3} =$

Answers – Day 3

Multiplying Mixed Numbers

1) $9\frac{8}{15}$

2) $11\frac{3}{8}$

3) $12\frac{3}{5}$

4) $3\frac{1}{18}$

5) $9\frac{2}{7}$

6) $20\frac{4}{9}$

7) $86\frac{19}{36}$

8) $13\frac{3}{7}$

9) $14\frac{1}{25}$

10) $14\frac{5}{21}$

Dividing Mixed Numbers

1) $\frac{1}{2}$

2) $1\frac{1}{2}$

3) $6\frac{3}{10}$

4) $\frac{19}{28}$

5) $1\frac{13}{20}$

6) $\frac{21}{26}$

7) $1\frac{1}{11}$

8) $\frac{57}{58}$

9) $3\frac{31}{48}$

10) $1\frac{19}{56}$

Day 4: Comparing and Rounding Decimals

Math Topics that you'll learn today:

- ✓ Comparing Decimals

- ✓ Rounding Decimals

Comparing Decimals

Step-by-step guide:

Decimals: is a fraction written in a special form. For example, instead of writing $\frac{1}{2}$ you can write **0.5**.

For comparing decimals:

- ✓ Compare each digit of two decimals in the same place value.
- ✓ Start from left. Compare hundreds, tens, ones, tenth, hundredth, etc.
- ✓ To compare numbers, use these symbols:
- - Equal to =,   Less than <,   Greater than >
    Greater than or equal ≥,   Less than or equal ≤

Examples:

1) Compare **0.20** and **0.02**.

   0.20 is greater than 0.02, because the tenth place of 0.20 is 2, but the tenth place of 0.02 is zero. Then: $0.20 > 0.02$

2) Compare **0.0210** and **0.110**.

   0.0.110 is greater than 0.0210, because the tenth place of 0.110 is 1, but the tenth place of 0.0210 is zero. Then: $0.0210 < 0.110$

✎ *Write the correct comparison symbol (>, < or =).*

1) 0.50 ☐ 0.050

2) 0.025 ☐ 0.25

3) 2.060 ☐ 2.07

4) 1.75 ☐ 1.07

5) 4.04 ☐ 0.440

6) 3.05 ☐ 3.5

7) 5.05 ☐ 5.050

8) 1.02 ☐ 1.1

9) 2.45 ☐ 2.125

10) 0.932 ☐ 0.0932

11) 3.15 ☐ 3.150

12) 0.718 ☐ 0.89

Rounding Decimals

Step-by-step guide:

- ✓ We can round decimals to a certain accuracy or number of decimal places. This is used to make calculation easier to do and results easier to understand, when exact values are not too important.
- ✓ First, you'll need to remember your place values: For example:

$$12.4567$$

1: tens	2: ones	4: tenths
5: hundredths	6: thousandths	7: tens thousandths

- ✓ To round a decimal, find the place value you'll round to.
- ✓ Find the digit to the right of the place value you're rounding to. If it is **5** or bigger, add **1** to the place value you're rounding to and remove all digits on its right side. If the digit to the right of the place value is less than **5**, keep the place value and remove all digits on the right.

Examples:

1) Round 2.1837 to the thousandth place value.

First look at the next place value to the right, (tens thousandths). It's 7 and it is greater than 5. Thus add 1 to the digit in the thousandth place.

Thousandth place is 3. → 3 + 1 = 4, then, the answer is 2.184

2) 2.1837 rounded to the nearest hundredth.

First look at the next place value to the right of thousandths. It's 3 and it is less than 5, thus remove all the digits to the right. Then, the answer is 2.18.

🖎 *Round each decimal to the nearest whole number.*

1) 23.18
2) 8.6
3) 14.45
4) 7.5
5) 3.95
6) 56.7

🖎 *Round each decimal to the nearest tenth.*

7) 22.652
8) 30.342
9) 47.847
10) 82.88
11) 16.184
12) 71.79

Answers – Day 4

Comparing Decimals

1) >

2) <

3) <

4) >

5) >

6) <

7) =

8) <

9) >

10) >

11) =

12) <

Rounding Decimals

1) 23

2) 9

3) 14

4) 8

5) 4

6) 57

7) 22.7

8) 30.3

9) 47.8

10) 82.9

11) 16.2

12) 71.8

Day 5: Decimal Operations

Math Topics that you'll learn today:

- ✓ Adding and Subtracting Decimals

- ✓ Multiplying and Dividing Decimals

Mathematics is no more computation than typing is literature.

~ John Allen Paulos

Adding and Subtracting Decimals

Step-by-step guide:

- ✓ Line up the numbers.

- ✓ Add zeros to have same number of digits for both numbers if necessary.

- ✓ Add or subtract using column addition or subtraction.

Examples:

1) Add. $2.5 + 1.24 =$

First line up the numbers: $\begin{array}{r} 2.5 \\ + 1.24 \\ \hline \end{array}$ → Add zeros to have same number of digits for both

numbers. $\begin{array}{r} 2.50 \\ + 1.24 \\ \hline \end{array}$, Start with the hundredths place. $0 + 4 = 4$, $\begin{array}{r} 2.50 \\ + 1.24 \\ \hline 4 \end{array}$, Continue with tenths

place. $5 + 2 = 7$, $\begin{array}{r} 2.50 \\ + 1.24 \\ \hline .74 \end{array}$. Add the ones place. $2 + 1 = 3$, $\begin{array}{r} 2.50 \\ + 1.24 \\ \hline 3.74 \end{array}$

2) Subtract decimals. $4.67 + 2.15 = \begin{array}{r} 4.67 \\ - 2.15 \\ \hline \end{array}$

Start with the hundredths place. $7 - 5 = 2$, $\begin{array}{r} 4.67 \\ - 2.15 \\ \hline 2 \end{array}$, continue with tenths place. $6 - 1 = 5$

$\begin{array}{r} 4.67 \\ - 2.15 \\ \hline .52 \end{array}$, subtract the ones place. $4 - 2 = 2$, $\begin{array}{r} 4.67 \\ - 2.15 \\ \hline 2.52 \end{array}$.

✍ *Find the sum or difference.*

1) $31.13 - 11.45 =$

2) $35.25 + 24.47 =$

3) $73.50 + 22.78 =$

4) $56.67 - 44.39 =$

5) $71.47 + 16.25 =$

6) $68.99 - 53.61 =$

7) $66.24 - 23.11 =$

8) $39.75 + 12.85 =$

Multiplying and Dividing Decimals

Step-by-step guide:

For Multiplication:

✓ Ignore the decimal point and set up and multiply the numbers as you do with whole numbers.
Count the total number of decimal places in both of the factors.
Place the decimal point in the product.
For Division:

✓ If the divisor is not a whole number, move decimal point to right to make it a whole number. Do the same for dividend.
✓ Divide similar to whole numbers.

Examples:

1) Find the product. $0.50 \times 0.20 =$

Set up and multiply the numbers as you do with whole numbers. Line up the numbers: $\begin{array}{r} 50 \\ \times 20 \\ \hline \end{array}$, Start with

the ones place $\rightarrow 50 \times 0 = 0$, $\begin{array}{r} 50 \\ \times 20 \\ \hline 0 \end{array}$, Continue with other digits $\rightarrow 50 \times 2 = 100$, $\begin{array}{r} 50 \\ \times 20 \\ \hline 1,000 \end{array}$, Count the

total number of decimal places in both of the factors. (4). Then Place the decimal point in the product.

Then: $\begin{array}{r} 0.50 \\ \times 0.20 \\ \hline 0.1000 \end{array}$ $\rightarrow 0.50 \times 0.20 = 0.1$

2) Find the quotient. $1.20 \div 0.2 =$

The divisor is not a whole number. Multiply it by 10 to get 2. Do the same for the dividend to get 12. Now, divide: $12 \div 2 = 6$. The answer is 6.

✎ Find the product and quotient.

1) $0.5 \times 0.4 =$

2) $2.5 \times 0.2 =$

3) $1.25 \times 0.5 =$

4) $0.75 \times 0.2 =$

5) $1.92 \times 0.8 =$

6) $0.55 \times 0.4 =$

7) $1.67 \div 100 =$

8) $52.2 \div 1,000 =$

9) $4.2 \div 2 =$

10) $8.6 \div 0.5 =$

11) $12.6 \div 0.2 =$

12) $16.5 \div 5 =$

Answers – Day 5

Adding and Subtracting Decimals

1) 19.68

2) 59.72

3) 96.28

4) 12.28

5) 87.72

6) 15.38

7) 43.13

8) 52.60

Multiplying and Dividing Decimals

1) 0.20

2) 0.50

3) 0.625

4) 0.15

5) 1.536

6) 0.22

7) 0.0167

8) 0.0522

9) 2.10

10) 17.2

11) 63

12) 3.3

Day 6: Factoring Numbers

Math Topics that you'll learn today:

- ✓ Factoring Numbers

- ✓ Greatest Common Factor

- ✓ Least Common Multiple

"The study of mathematics, like the Nile, begins in minuteness but ends in magnificence."

- Charles Caleb Colton

Factoring Numbers

Step-by-step guide:

- ✓ Factoring numbers means to break the numbers into their prime factors.
- ✓ First few prime numbers: $2, 3, 5, 7, 11, 13, 17, 19$

Examples:

1) List all positive factors of **12**.

     Write the upside-down division:
     The second column is the answer.
     Then: $12 = 2 \times 2 \times 3$ or $12 = 2^2 \times 3$

12	2
6	2
3	3
1	

2) List all positive factors of **20**.

     Write the upside-down division:
     The second column is the answer.
     Then: $20 = 2 \times 2 \times 5$ or $20 = 2^2 \times 5$

20	2
10	2
5	5
1	

✎ *List all positive factors of each number.*

1) 8	5) 25	9) 42
2) 9	6) 28	10) 48
3) 15	7) 26	11) 50
4) 16	8) 35	12) 36

Greatest Common Factor

Step-by-step guide:

- ✓ List the prime factors of each number.
- ✓ Multiply common prime factors.
- ✓ If there are no common prime factors, the GCF is **1**.

Examples:

1) Find the GCF for **10** and **15**.

The factors of 10 are: $\{1, 2, 5, 10\}$

The factors of 15 are: $\{1, 3, 5, 15\}$

There is 5 in common,

Then the greatest common factor is: 5.

2) Find the GCF for **8** and **20**.

The factors of 8 are: $\{1, 2, 4, 8\}$

The factors of 20 are: $\{1, 2, 4, 5, 10, 20\}$

There is 2 and 4 in common.

Then the greatest common factor is: $2 \times 4 = 8$.

✍ *Find the GCF for each number pair.*

1) $4, 2$ 5) $5, 10$ 9) $5, 12$

2) $3, 5$ 6) $6, 12$ 10) $4, 14$

3) $2, 6$ 7) $7, 14$ 11) $15, 18$

4) $4, 7$ 8) $6, 14$ 12) $12, 20$

Least Common Multiple

Step-by-step guide:

- ✓ Least Common Multiple is the smallest multiple that 2 or more numbers have in common.
- ✓ How to find LCM: list out all the multiples of each number and then find the first one they have in common.

Examples:

1) Find the LCM for **3** and **4**.

Multiples of 3: $3, 6, 9, 12, 15, 18, 21, 24$

Multiples of 4: $4, 8, 12, 16, 20, 24$

$LCM = 12$

2) Find the LCM for **9** and **12**.

Multiples of 9: $9, 18, 27, 36, 45$

Multiples of 12: $12, 24, 36, 48$

$LCM = 36$

✎ *Find the LCM for each number pair.*

1) 3, 6	5) 6, 18	9) 4, 18
2) 5, 10	6) 10, 12	10) 9, 12
3) 6, 14	7) 4, 12	11) 12, 16
4) 8, 9	8) 5, 15	12) 15, 18

Answers – Day 6

Factoring Numbers

1) 1, 2, 4, 8

2) 1, 3, 9

3) 1, 3, 5, 15

4) 1, 2, 4, 8, 16

5) 1, 5, 25

6) 1, 2, 4, 7, 14, 28

7) 1, 2, 13, 26

8) 1, 5, 7, 35

9) 1, 2, 3, 6, 7, 14, 21, 42

10) 1, 2, 3, 4, 6, 8, 12, 16, 24, 48

11) 1, 2, 5, 10, 25, 50

12) 1, 2, 3, 4, 6, 9, 12, 18, 36

Greatest Common Factor

1) 2

2) 1

3) 2

4) 1

5) 5

6) 12

7) 7

8) 2

9) 1

10) 2

11) 3

12) 4

Least Common Multiple

1) 6

2) 10

3) 42

4) 72

5) 18

6) 60

7) 12

8) 15

9) 36

10) 36

11) 48

12) 90

Day 7: Integers

Math Topics that you'll learn today:

- ✓ Adding and Subtracting Integers

- ✓ Multiplying and Dividing Integers

- ✓ Ordering Integers and Numbers

Without mathematics, there's nothing you can do. Everything around you is mathematics. Everything around you is numbers." – Shakuntala Devi

Adding and Subtracting Integers

Step-by-step guide:

- ✓ Integers includes: zero, counting numbers, and the negative of the counting numbers. $\{... , -3, -2, -1, 0, 1, 2, 3, ...\}$
- ✓ Add a positive integer by moving to the right on the number line.
- ✓ Add a negative integer by moving to the left on the number line.
- ✓ Subtract an integer by adding its opposite.

Examples:

1) Solve. $(-8) - (-5) =$

Keep the first number, and convert the sign of the second number to it's opposite. (change subtraction into addition. Then: $(-8) + 5 = -3$

2) Solve. $10 + (4 - 8) =$

First subtract the numbers in brackets, $4 - 8 = -4$

Then: $10 + (-4) = \rightarrow$ change addition into subtraction: $10 - 4 = 6$

✍ *Find each sum or difference.*

1) $12 + (-5) =$

2) $(-14) + (-18) =$

3) $8 + (-28) =$

4) $43 + (-12) =$

5) $(-7) + (-11) + 4 =$

6) $37 + (-16) + 12 =$

7) $(-12) - (-8) =$

8) $15 - (-20) =$

9) $(-11) - 25 =$

10) $30 - (-16) =$

11) $56 - (45 - 23) =$

12) $15 - (-4) - (-34) =$

Multiplying and Dividing Integers

Step-by-step guide:

Use these rules for multiplying and dividing integers:
- ✓ (negative) × (negative) = positive
- ✓ (negative) ÷ (negative) = positive
- ✓ (negative) × (positive) = negative
- ✓ (negative) ÷ (positive) = negative
- ✓ (positive) × (positive) = positive

Examples:

1) Solve. $(2 - 5) \times (3) =$

First subtract the numbers in brackets, $2 - 5 = -3 \rightarrow (-3) \times (3) =$

Now use this formula: (negative) × (positive) = negative
$(-3) \times (3) = -9$

2) Solve. $(-12) + (48 \div 6) =$

First divided 48 by 6 , the numbers in brackets, $48 \div 6 = 8$

$(-12) + (8) = -12 + 8 = -4$

✍ *Find each product or quotient.*

1) $(-7) \times (-8) =$

2) $(-4) \times 5 =$

3) $5 \times (-11) =$

4) $(-5) \times (-20) =$

5) $-(2) \times (-8) \times 3 =$

6) $(12 - 4) \times (-10) =$

7) $16 \div (-4) =$

8) $(-25) \div (-5) =$

9) $(-40) \div (-8) =$

10) $64 \div (-8) =$

11) $(-49) \div 7 =$

12) $(-112) \div (-4) =$

Ordering Integers and Numbers

Step-by-step guide:

✓ When using a number line, numbers increase as you move to the right.
✓ When comparing two numbers, think about their position on number line. If one number is on the right side of another number, it is a bigger number. For example, -3 is bigger than -5 because it is on the right side of -5 on number line.

Examples:

1) Order this set of integers from least to greatest. $-2, 1, -5, -1, 2, 4$
The smallest number is -5 and the largest number is 4.

Now compare the integers and order them from greatest to least:
$-5 < -2 < -1 < 1 < 2 < 4$

2) Order each set of integers from greatest to least. $10, -6, -2, 5, -8, 4$
The largest number is 10 and the smallest number is -8.

Now compare the integers and order them from least to greatest:
$10 > 5 > 4 > -2 > -6 > -8$

✎ *Order each set of integers from least to greatest.*

1) $7, -9, -6, -1, 3$ ___, ___, ___, ___, ___, ___
2) $-4, -11, 5, 12, 9$ ___, ___, ___, ___, ___, ___
3) $18, -12, -19, 21, -20$ ___, ___, ___, ___, ___, ___
4) $-15, -25, 18, -7, 32$ ___, ___, ___, ___, ___, ___

✎ *Order each set of integers from greatest to least.*

5) $11, 16, -9, -12, -4$ ___, ___, ___, ___, ___, ___
6) $23, 31, -14, -20, 39$ ___, ___, ___, ___, ___, ___
7) $45, -21, -18, 55, -5$ ___, ___, ___, ___, ___, ___
8) $68, 81, -14, -10, 94$ ___, ___, ___, ___, ___, ___

Answers – Day 7

Adding and Subtracting Integers

1) 7
2) −32
3) −20
4) 31
5) −14
6) 33

7) −4
8) 35
9) −36
10) 46
11) 34
12) 53

Multiplying and Dividing Integers

1) 56
2) −20
3) −55
4) 100
5) 48
6) −80

7) −4
8) 5
9) 5
10) −8
11) −7
12) 28

Ordering Integers and Numbers

1) −9, −6, −1, 3, 7
2) −11, −4, 5, 9, 12
3) −20, −19, −12, 18, 21
4) −25, −15, −7, 18, 32

5) 16, 11, −4, −9, −12
6) 39, 31, 23, −14, −20
7) 55, 45, −5, −18, −21
8) 94, 81, 68, −10, −14

Day 8: Order of Operations and Absolute value

Math Topics that you'll learn today:

✓ Order of Operations

✓ Integers and Absolute Value

"Sometimes the questions are complicated and the answers are simple." ~ Dr. Seuss

Order of Operations

Step-by-step guide:

When there is more than one math operation, use PEMDAS:

✓ Parentheses

✓ Exponents

✓ Multiplication and Division (from left to right)

✓ Addition and Subtraction (from left to right)

Examples:

1) Solve. $(5 + 7) \div (3^2 \div 3) =$

First simplify inside parentheses: $(12) \div (9 \div 3) = (12) \div (3) =$
Then: $(12) \div (3) = 4$

2) Solve. $(11 \times 5) - (12 - 7) =$

First simplify inside parentheses: $(11 \times 5) - (12 - 7) = (55) - (5) =$

Then: $(55) - (5) = 50$

✍ *Evaluate each expression.*

1) $5 + (4 \times 2) =$

2) $13 - (2 \times 5) =$

3) $(16 \times 2) + 18 =$

4) $(12 - 5) - (4 \times 3) =$

5) $25 + (14 \div 2) =$

6) $(18 \times 5) \div 5 =$

7) $(48 \div 2) \times (-4) =$

8) $(7 \times 5) + (25 - 12) =$

9) $64 + (3 \times 2) + 8 =$

10) $(20 \times 5) \div (4 + 1) =$

11) $(-9) + (12 \times 6) + 15 =$

12) $(7 \times 8) - (56 \div 4) =$

Integers and Absolute Value

Step-by-step guide:

✓ To find an absolute value of a number, just find its distance from **0** on number line! For example, the distance of **12** and **−12** from zero on number line is **12**!

Examples:

1) Solve. $\frac{|-18|}{9} \times |5 - 8| =$

First find $| - 18|$, →the absolute value of −18 is 18, then: $|-18| = 18$

$\frac{18}{9} \times |5 - 8| =$

Next, solve $|5 - 8|$, → $|5 - 8| = |-3|$, the absolute value of −3 is 3. $|-3| = 3$

Then: $\frac{18}{9} \times 3 = 2 \times 3 = 6$

2) Solve. $|10 - 5| \times \frac{|-2\times6|}{3} =$

First solve $|10 - 5|$, → $|10 - 5| = |5|$, the absolute value of 5 is 5, $|5| = 5$

$5 \times \frac{|-2\times6|}{3} =$

Now solve $|-2 \times 6|$, → $|-2 \times 6| = |-12|$, the absolute value of −12 is 12, $|-12| = 12$

Then: $5 \times \frac{12}{3} = 5 \times 4 = 20$

✎ *Evaluate the value.*

1) $8 - |2 - 14| - |-2| =$

2) $|-2| - \frac{|-10|}{2} =$

3) $\frac{|-36|}{6} \times |-6| =$

4) $\frac{|5 \times -3|}{5} \times \frac{|-20|}{4} =$

5) $|2 \times -4| + \frac{|-40|}{5} =$

6) $\frac{|-28|}{4} \times \frac{|-55|}{11} =$

7) $| - 12 + 4| \times \frac{|-4\times5|}{2} =$

8) $\frac{|-10 \times 3|}{2} \times |-12| =$

Answers – Day 8

Order of Operations

1) 13

2) 3

3) 50

4) −5

5) 32

6) 18

7) −96

8) 48

9) 78

10) 20

11) 78

12) 42

Integers and Absolute Value

1) −6

2) −3

3) 36

4) 15

5) 16

6) 35

7) 80

8) 180

Day 9: Ratios

Math Topics that you'll learn today:

- ✓ Simplifying Ratios

- ✓ Proportional Ratios

Simplifying Ratios

Step-by-step guide:

- ✓ Ratios are used to make comparisons between two numbers.
- ✓ Ratios can be written as a fraction, using the word "to", or with a colon.
- ✓ You can calculate equivalent ratios by multiplying or dividing both sides of the ratio by the same number.

Examples:

1) Simplify. $8:4 =$

Both numbers 8 and 4 are divisible by 4 , $\Rightarrow$ $8 \div 4 = 2, 4 \div 4 = 1,$

Then: $8:4 = 2:1$

2) Simplify. $\dfrac{12}{36} =$

Both numbers 12 and 36 are divisible by 12, $\Rightarrow$ $12 \div 12 = 1, 36 \div 12 = 3,$

Then: $\dfrac{12}{36} = \dfrac{1}{3}$

✎ *Reduce each ratio.*

1) $12:8 = \underline{\quad}:\underline{\quad}$

2) $2:20 = \underline{\quad}:\underline{\quad}$

3) $3:36 = \underline{\quad}:\underline{\quad}$

4) $8:16 = \underline{\quad}:\underline{\quad}$

5) $6:100 = \underline{\quad}:\underline{\quad}$

6) $10:60 = \underline{\quad}:\underline{\quad}$

7) $21:49 = \underline{\quad}:\underline{\quad}$

8) $20:40 = \underline{\quad}:\underline{\quad}$

9) $10:50 = \underline{\quad}:\underline{\quad}$

10) $14:18 = \underline{\quad}:\underline{\quad}$

11) $45:27 = \underline{\quad}:\underline{\quad}$

12) $49:21 = \underline{\quad}:\underline{\quad}$

Proportional Ratios

Step-by-step guide:

✓ A proportion means that two ratios are equal. It can be written in two ways:
$$\frac{a}{b} = \frac{c}{d} , \ a : b = c : d$$

✓ The proportion $\frac{a}{b} = \frac{c}{d}$ can be written as: $a \times d = c \times b$

Examples:

1) Solve this proportion for x. $\frac{4}{8} = \frac{5}{x}$

Use cross multiplication: $\frac{4}{8} = \frac{5}{x} \Rightarrow 4 \times x = 5 \times 8 \Rightarrow 4x = 40$

Divide to find x: $x = \frac{40}{4} \Rightarrow x = 10$

2) If a box contains red and blue balls in ratio of $2 : 3$ red to blue, how many red balls are there if **90** blue balls are in the box?

Write a proportion and solve. $\frac{2}{3} = \frac{x}{90}$

Use cross multiplication: $2 \times 90 = 3 \times x \Rightarrow 180 = 3x$

Divide to find x: $x = \frac{180}{3} \Rightarrow x = 60$

✎ *Solve each proportion.*

1) $\frac{2}{5} = \frac{14}{x}, x = $ _____

2) $\frac{1}{6} = \frac{7}{x}, x = $ _____

3) $\frac{3}{5} = \frac{27}{x}, x = $ _____

4) $\frac{1}{5} = \frac{x}{80}, x = $ _____

5) $\frac{3}{7} = \frac{x}{63}, x = $ _____

6) $\frac{1}{4} = \frac{13}{x}, x = $ _____

7) $\frac{7}{9} = \frac{56}{x}, x = $ _____

8) $\frac{6}{11} = \frac{42}{x}, x = $ _____

9) $\frac{4}{7} = \frac{x}{77}, x = $ _____

10) $\frac{5}{13} = \frac{x}{143}, x = $ _____

11) $\frac{7}{19} = \frac{x}{209}, x = $ _____

12) $\frac{3}{13} = \frac{x}{195}, x = $ _____

Answers – Day 9

Simplifying Ratios

1) 3 : 2
2) 1 : 10
3) 1 : 12
4) 1 : 2
5) 3 : 50
6) 1 : 6

7) 3 : 7
8) 1 : 2
9) 1 : 5
10) 7 : 9
11) 5 : 3
12) 7 : 3

Proportional Ratios

1) 35
2) 42
3) 45
4) 16
5) 27
6) 52

7) 72
8) 77
9) 44
10) 55
11) 77
12) 45

Day 10: Similarity and Proportions

Math Topics that you'll learn today:

- ✓ Create a Proportion

- ✓ Similarity and Ratios

- ✓ Simple Interest

Mathematics - the unshaken Foundation of Sciences, and the plentiful Fountain of Advantage to human affairs. ~

Isaac Barrow

Create a Proportion

Step-by-step guide:

- ✓ A proportion contains two equal fractions! A proportion simply means that two fractions are equal.
- ✓ To create a proportion, simply find (or create) two equal fractions.

Examples:

1) Express ratios as a Proportion.

120 miles on **4** gallons of gas, how many miles on **1** gallon of gas?

First create a fraction: $\frac{120\ miles}{4\ gallons}$, and divide: $120 \div 4 = 30$

Then: 30 miles per gallon

2) State if this pair of ratios form a proportion. $\frac{3}{5}$ and $\frac{24}{45}$

Use cross multiplication: $\frac{3}{5} = \frac{24}{45} \rightarrow 3 \times 45 = 5 \times 24 \rightarrow 135 = 120$, which is not correct. Therefore, this pair of ratios doesn't form a proportion.

✎ *State if each pair of ratios form a proportion.*

1) $\frac{3}{10}$ and $\frac{9}{30}$

2) $\frac{1}{2}$ and $\frac{16}{32}$

3) $\frac{5}{6}$ and $\frac{35}{42}$

4) $\frac{3}{7}$ and $\frac{27}{72}$

5) $\frac{2}{5}$ and $\frac{16}{45}$

6) $\frac{4}{9}$ and $\frac{40}{81}$

7) $\frac{6}{11}$ and $\frac{42}{77}$

8) $\frac{1}{6}$ and $\frac{8}{48}$

9) $\frac{6}{17}$ and $\frac{36}{85}$

10) $\frac{2}{7}$ and $\frac{24}{86}$

11) $\frac{12}{19}$ and $\frac{156}{247}$

12) $\frac{13}{21}$ and $\frac{182}{294}$

Similarity and Ratios

Step-by-step guide:

✓ Two or more figures are similar if the corresponding angles are equal, and the corresponding sides are in proportion.

Examples:

1) A girl **160** *cm* tall, stands **360** *cm* from a lamp post at night. Her shadow from the light is **90** *cm* long. How high is the lamp post?

Write the proportion and solve for missing side.

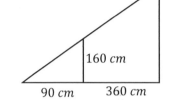

$$\frac{Smaller\ triangle\ height}{Smaller\ triangle\ base} = \frac{Bigger\ triangle\ height}{Bigger\ triangle\ base}$$

$$\Rightarrow \frac{90\ cm}{160\ cm} = \frac{90+360\ cm}{x} \Rightarrow 90x = 160 \times 450 \Rightarrow x = 800\ cm$$

2) A tree **32** feet tall casts a shadow **12** feet long. Jack is **6** feet tall. How long is Jack's shadow?

Write a proportion and solve for the missing number.

$$\frac{32}{12} = \frac{6}{x} \rightarrow 32x = 6 \times 12$$

$$32x = 72 \rightarrow x = \frac{72}{32} = 2.25$$

✎ **Solve.**

1) Two rectangles are similar. The first is 6 *feet* wide and 20 feet long. The second is 15 feet wide. What is the length of the second rectangle? _____

2) Two rectangles are similar. One is 2.5 meters by 9 meters. The longer side of the second rectangle is 22.5 meters. What is the other side of the second rectangle? _____

3) A building casts a shadow 24 *ft* long. At the same time a girl 5 *ft* tall casts a shadow 2 *ft* long. How tall is the building? _____

4) The scale of a map of Texas is 2 inches: 45 miles. If you measure the distance from Dallas to Martin County as 14.4 inches, approximately how far is Martin County from Dallas? _____

Simple Interest

Step-by-step guide:

✓ Simple Interest: The charge for borrowing money or the return for lending it. To solve a simple interest problem, use this formula:

Interest = principal x rate x time ⇒ $I = p \times r \times t$

Examples:

1) Find simple interest for $**450** investment at **7%** for **8** years.

Use Interest formula: $I = prt$

$p = \$450, r = 7\% = \dfrac{7}{100} = 0.07$ and $t = 8$

Then: $I = 450 \times 0.07 \times 8 = \$252$

2) Find simple interest for $**5,200** at **4%** for **3** years.

Use Interest formula: $I = prt$

$p = \$5,200, r = 4\% = \dfrac{4}{100} = 0.04$ and $t = 3$

Then: $I = 5,200 \times 0.04 \times 3 = \$624$

✎ *Determine the simple interest for these loans.*

1) $1,300 at 5% for 6 years. $ _____

2) $5,400 at 3.5% for 6 months. $ _____

3) $600 at 4% for 9 months. $ _____

4) $24,000 at 5.5% for 5 years. $ _____

5) $15,600 at 3% for 2 years. $ _____

6) $1,200 at 5.5% for 4 years. $ _____

7) $1,600 at 4.5% for 9 months. $ _____

8) $12,000 at 2.2% for 5 years. $ _____

Answers – Day 10

Create a Proportion

1) Yes

2) Yes

3) Yes

4) No

5) No

6) No

7) Yes

8) Yes

9) No

10) No

11) Yes

12) Yes

Similarity and ratios

1) 50 feet

2) 6.25 meters

3) 60 feet

4) 324 miles

Simple Interest

1) $390.00

2) $94.50

3) $18.00

4) $6,600.00

5) $936.00

6) $264.00

7) $54

8) $1,320.00

Day 11: Percentage

Math Topics that you'll learn today:

- ✓ Percentage Calculations

- ✓ Percent Problems

Mathematics is no more computation than typing is literature.

– John Allen Paulos

Percentage Calculations

Step-by-step guide:

- ✓ Percent is a ratio of a number and **100**. It always has the same denominator, 100. Percent symbol is %.
- ✓ Percent is another way to write decimals or fractions. For example:

$$40\% = 0.40 = \frac{40}{100} = \frac{2}{5}$$

- ✓ Use the following formula to find part, whole, or percent:

$$part = \frac{percent}{100} \times whole$$

Examples:

1) What is **10%** of 45? Use the following formula: $part = \frac{percent}{100} \times whole$

$$part = \frac{10}{100} \times 45 \rightarrow part = \frac{1}{10} \times 45 \rightarrow part = \frac{45}{10} \rightarrow part = 4.5$$

2) What is **15%** of 24? Use the percent formula: $part = \frac{percent}{100} \times whole$

$$part = \frac{15}{100} \times 24 \rightarrow part = \frac{360}{100} \rightarrow part = 3.6$$

✍ *Calculate the given percent of each value.*

1) 2% of 50 = ____

2) 10% of 30 = ____

3) 20% of 25 = ____

4) 50% of 80 = ____

5) 40% of 200 = ____

6) 20% of 45 = ____

7) 35% of 20 = ____

8) 12% of 400 = ____

9) 40% of 90 = ____

10) 25% of 812 = ____

11) 32% of 600 = ____

12) 87% of 500 = ____

Percent Problems

Step-by-step guide:

- ✓ In each percent problem, we are looking for the base, or part or the percent.
- ✓ Use the following equations to find each missing section.
    - ○ Base = Part ÷ Percent
    - ○ Part = Percent × Base
    - ○ Percent = Part ÷ Base

Examples:

1) **1.2 is what percent of 24?**

In this problem, we are looking for the percent. Use the following equation:
$$Percent = Part \div Base \rightarrow Percent = 1.2 \div 24 = 0.05 = 5\%$$

2) **20 is 5% of what number?**

Use the following formula: $Base = Part \div Percent \rightarrow Base = 20 \div 0.05 = 400$
20 is 5% of 400.

✍ *Solve each problem.*

1) 20 is what percent of 50? ____%

2) 18 is what percent of 90? ____%

3) 12 is what percent of 15? ____%

4) 16 is what percent of 200? ____%

5) 24 is what percent of 800? ____%

6) 48 is what percent of 400? ____%

7) 90 is 12 percent of what number? ____

8) 24 is 8 percent of what? ____

9) 60 is 15 percent of what number? ____

10) 42 *is 12 percent of what?* ____

11) 11 *is 25 percent of what?* ____

12) 8 *is 12.5 percent of what?* ____

Answers – Day 11

Percentage Calculations

1) 1

2) 3

3) 5

4) 40

5) 80

6) 9

7) 7

8) 48

9) 36

10) 203

11) 192

12) 435

Percent Problems

1) 40%

2) 20%

3) 80%

4) 8%

5) 3%

6) 12%

7) 750

8) 300

9) 400

10) 350

11) 44

12) 64

Day 12: Percent of Change

Math Topics that you'll learn today:

- ✓ Percent of Increase and Decrease

- ✓ Discount, Tax and Tip

Mathematics is a great motivator for all humans. Because its career starts with zero and it never end (infinity).

Percent of Increase and Decrease

Step-by-step guide:

To find the percentage of increase or decrease:
- ✓ New Number – Original Number
- ✓ The result ÷ Original Number × 100
- ✓ If your answer is a negative number, then this is a percentage decrease. If it is positive, then this is a percent of increase.

Examples:

1) Increased by **50**%, the numbers **84** becomes:

   First find 50% of 84 $\rightarrow \frac{50}{100} \times 84 = \frac{50 \times 84}{100} = 42$

   Then: $84 + 42 = 126$

2) The price of a shirt increases from **$10** to **$14**. What is the percent increase?
   First: $14 - 10 = 4$

   4 is the result. Then: $4 \div 10 = \frac{4}{10} = 0.4 = 40\%$

✎ *Solve each percent of change word problem.*

1) Bob got a raise, and his hourly wage increased from $12 to $15. What is the percent increase? _____ %

2) The price of a pair of shoes increases from $20 to $32. What is the percent increase? _____ %

3) At a coffeeshop, the price of a cup of coffee increased from $1.20 to $1.44. What is the percent increase in the cost of the coffee? _____ %

4) 6 *cm* are cut from a 24 *cm* board. What is the percent decrease in length? _____ %

5) In a class, the number of students has been increased from 18 to 27. What is the percent increase? _____ %

6) The price of gasoline rose from $2.40 to $2.76 in one month. By what percent did the gas price rise? _____ %

7) A shirt was originally priced at $48. It went on sale for $38.40. What was the percent that the shirt was discounted? _____ %

Discount, Tax and Tip

Step-by-step guide:

- ✓ Discount = Multiply the regular price by the rate of discount
- ✓ Selling price = original price – discount
- ✓ Tax: To find tax, multiply the tax rate to the taxable amount (income, property value, etc.)
- ✓ To find tip, multiply the rate to the selling price.

Examples:

1) With an **10**% discount, Ella was able to save $**20** on a dress. What was the original price of the dress?

$10\% \ of \ x = \ 20, \frac{10}{100} \times x = \ 20, x = \frac{100 \times 20}{10} = 200$

2) Sophia purchased a sofa for $**530.40**. The sofa is regularly priced at $**624**. What was the percent discount Sophia received on the sofa?

Use this formula: $percent = Part \div base = 530.40 \div 624 = 0.85 = 85\%$

Therefore, the discount is: $100\% - 85\% = 15\%$

✎ *Find the selling price of each item.*

1) Original price of a computer: $500

  Tax: 6%, Selling price: $_____

2) Original price of a laptop: $350

  Tax: 8%, Selling price: $_____

3) Original price of a sofa: $800

  Tax: 7%, Selling price: $_____

4) Original price of a car: $18,500

  Tax: 8.5%, Selling price: $_____

5) Original price of a Table: $250

  Tax: 5%, Selling price: $_____

6) Original price of a house: $250,000

  Tax: 6.5% Selling price: $_____

7) Original price of a tablet: $400

  Discount: 20%, Selling price: $_____

8) Original price of a chair: $150

  Discount: 15%, Selling price: $_____

9) Original price of a book: $50

  Discount: 25%, Selling price: $_____

10) Original price of a cellphone: $500

  Discount: 10%, Selling price: $_____

Answers – Day 12

Percent of Increase and Decrease

1) 25%

2) 60%

3) 20%

4) 25%

5) 50%

6) 15%

7) 20%

Markup, Discount, and Tip

1) $530.00

2) $378.00

3) $856.00

4) $20,072.50

5) $262.50

6) $266,250

7) $320.00

8) $127.50

9) $37.50

10) $450.00

Day 13: Exponents and Variables

Math Topics that you'll learn today:

- ✓ Multiplication Property of Exponents

- ✓ Division Property of Exponents

Multiplication Property of Exponents

Step-by-step guide:

- ✓ Exponents are shorthand for repeated multiplication of the same number by itself. For example, instead of 2×2, we can write 2^2. For $3 \times 3 \times 3 \times 3$, we can write 3^4
- ✓ In algebra, a variable is a letter used to stand for a number. The most common letters are: $x, y, z, a, b, c, m,$ and n.
- ✓ Exponent's rules: $x^a \times x^b = x^{a+b}$, $\frac{x^a}{x^b} = x^{a-b}$

$$(x^a)^b = x^{a \times b}, \qquad (xy)^a = x^a \times y^a , \left(\frac{a}{b}\right)^c = \frac{a^c}{b^c}$$

Examples:

1) Multiply. $-2x^5 \times 7x^3 =$

Use Exponent's rules: $x^a \times x^b = x^{a+b} \rightarrow x^5 \times x^3 = x^{5+3} = x^8$

Then: $-2x^5 \times 7x^3 = -14x^8$

2) Multiply. $(x^2 y^4)^3 =$

Use Exponent's rules: $(x^a)^b = x^{a \times b}$. Then: $(x^2 y^4)^3 = x^{2 \times 3} y^{4 \times 3} = x^6 y^{12}$

✎ *Simplify and write the answer in exponential form.*

1) $x^4 \times 3x =$

2) $x \times 2x^2 =$

3) $5x^4 \times 5x^4 =$

4) $2yx^2 \times 2x =$

5) $3x^4 \times y^2 x^4 =$

6) $y^2 x^3 \times y^5 x^2 =$

7) $4yx^3 \times 2x^2 y^3 =$

8) $6x^2 \times 6x^3 y^4 =$

9) $3x^4 y^5 \times 7x^2 y^3 =$

10) $7x^2 y^5 \times 9xy^3 =$

11) $7xy^4 \times 4x^3 y^3 =$

12) $3x^5 y^3 \times 8x^2 y^3 =$

Division Property of Exponents

Step-by-step guide:

✓ For division of exponents use these formulas: $\frac{x^a}{x^b} = x^{a-b}$, $x \neq 0$

$$\frac{x^a}{x^b} = \frac{1}{x^{b-a}}, x \neq 0, \qquad \frac{1}{x^b} = x^{-b}$$

Examples:

1) Simplify. $\frac{4x^3y}{36x^2y^3} =$

First cancel the common factor: $4 \rightarrow \frac{4x^3y}{36x^2y^3} = \frac{x^3y}{9x^2y^3}$

Use Exponent's rules: $\frac{x^a}{x^b} = x^{a-b} \rightarrow \frac{x^3}{x^2} = x^{3-2} = x$

Then: $\frac{4x^3y}{36x^2y^3} = \frac{xy}{9y^3} \rightarrow$ now cancel the common factor: $y \rightarrow \frac{xy}{9y^3} = \frac{x}{9y^2}$

2) Divide. $\frac{2x^{-5}}{9x^{-2}} =$

Use Exponent's rules: $\frac{x^a}{x^b} = \frac{1}{x^{b-a}} \rightarrow \frac{x^{-5}}{x^{-2}} = \frac{1}{x^{-2-(-5)}} = \frac{1}{x^{-2+5}} = \frac{1}{x^3}$

Then: $\frac{2x^{-5}}{9x^{-2}} = \frac{2}{9x^3}$

✎ Simplify.

1) $\frac{3^4 \times 3^7}{3^2 \times 3^8} =$

2) $\frac{5x}{10x^3} =$

3) $\frac{3x^3}{2x^5} =$

4) $\frac{12x^3}{14x^6} =$

5) $\frac{12x^3}{9y^8} =$

6) $\frac{25xy^4}{5x^6y^2} =$

7) $\frac{2x^4}{7x} =$

8) $\frac{16x^2y^8}{4x^3} =$

9) $\frac{12x^4}{15x^7y^9} =$

10) $\frac{12yx^4}{10yx^8} =$

11) $\frac{16x^4y}{9x^8y^2} =$

12) $\frac{5x^8}{20x^8} =$

Answers – Day 13

Multiplication Property of Exponents

1) $3x^5$

2) $2x^3$

3) $25x^8$

4) $4x^3y$

5) $3x^8y^2$

6) x^5y^7

7) $8x^5y^4$

8) $36x^5y^4$

9) $21x^6y^8$

10) $63x^3y^8$

11) $28x^4y^7$

12) $24x^7y^6$

Division Property of Exponents

1) 3

2) $\dfrac{1}{2x^2}$

3) $\dfrac{3}{2x^2}$

4) $\dfrac{6}{7x^3}$

5) $\dfrac{4x^3}{3y^8}$

6) $\dfrac{5y^2}{x^5}$

7) $\dfrac{2x^3}{7}$

8) $\dfrac{4y^8}{x}$

9) $\dfrac{4}{5x^3y^9}$

10) $\dfrac{6}{5x^4}$

11) $\dfrac{16}{9x^4y}$

12) $\dfrac{1}{4}$

Day 14: Exponents and Roots

Math Topics that you'll learn today:

- ✓ Powers of Products and Quotients

- ✓ Zero and Negative Exponents

Mathematics is no more computation than typing is literature.

- John Allen Paulos

Powers of Products and Quotients

Step-by-step guide:

✓ For any nonzero numbers a and b and any integer x, $(ab)^x = a^x \times b^x$.

Example:

1) Simplify. $(3x^5y^4)^2 =$

Use Exponent's rules: $(x^a)^b = x^{a \times b}$

$(3x^5y^4)^2 = (3)^2(x^5)^2(y^4)^2 = 9x^{5 \times 2}y^{4 \times 2} = 9x^{10}y^8$

2) Simplify. $\left(\frac{2x}{3x^2}\right)^2 =$

First cancel the common factor: $x \rightarrow \left(\frac{2x}{3x^2}\right)^2 = \left(\frac{2}{3x}\right)^2$

Use Exponent's rules: $\left(\frac{a}{b}\right)^c = \frac{a^c}{b^c}$

Then: $\left(\frac{2}{3x}\right)^2 = \frac{2^2}{(3x)^2} = \frac{4}{9x^2}$

✍ *Simplify.*

1) $(4x^3x^3)^2 =$

2) $(3x^3 \times 5x)^2 =$

3) $(10x^{11}y^3)^2 =$

4) $(9x^7y^5)^2 =$

5) $(4x^4y^6)^5 =$

6) $(3x \times 4y^3)^2 =$

7) $\left(\frac{5x}{x^2}\right)^2 =$

8) $\left(\frac{x^4y^4}{x^2y^2}\right)^3 =$

9) $\left(\frac{25x}{5x^6}\right)^2 =$

10) $\left(\frac{x^8}{x^6y^2}\right)^2 =$

11) $\left(\frac{xy^2}{x^3y^3}\right)^{-2} =$

12) $\left(\frac{2xy^4}{x^3}\right)^2 =$

Zero and Negative Exponents

Step-by-step guide:

✓ A negative exponent simply means that the base is on the wrong side of the fraction line, so you need to flip the base to the other side. For instance, "x^{-2}" (pronounced as "ecks to the minus two") just means "x^2" but underneath, as in $\frac{1}{x^2}$.

Example:

1) Evaluate. $\left(\frac{4}{9}\right)^{-2} =$

Use Exponent's rules: $\frac{1}{x^b} = x^{-b} \rightarrow \left(\frac{4}{9}\right)^{-2} = \frac{1}{\left(\frac{4}{9}\right)^2} = \frac{1}{\frac{4^2}{9^2}}$

Now use fraction rule: $\frac{1}{\frac{b}{c}} = \frac{c}{b} \rightarrow \frac{1}{\frac{4^2}{9^2}} = \frac{9^2}{4^2} = \frac{81}{16}$

2) Evaluate. $\left(\frac{5}{6}\right)^{-3} =$

Use Exponent's rules: $\frac{1}{x^b} = x^{-b} \rightarrow \left(\frac{5}{6}\right)^{-3} = \frac{1}{\left(\frac{5}{6}\right)^3} = \frac{1}{\frac{5^3}{6^3}}$

Now use fraction rule: $\frac{1}{\frac{b}{c}} = \frac{c}{b} \rightarrow \frac{1}{\frac{5^3}{6^3}} = \frac{6^3}{5^3} = \frac{216}{125}$

✍ *Evaluate the following expressions.*

1) $2^{-3} =$

2) $3^{-3} =$

3) $7^{-3} =$

4) $6^{-3} =$

5) $8^{-3} =$

6) $9^{-2} =$

7) $10^{-3} =$

8) $10^{-9} =$

9) $\left(\frac{1}{2}\right)^{-1}$

10) $\left(\frac{1}{2}\right)^{-2} =$

11) $\left(\frac{1}{3}\right)^{-2} =$

12) $\left(\frac{2}{3}\right)^{-2} =$

Answers – Day 14

Powers of Products and Quotients

1) $16x^{12}$

2) $225x^8$

3) $100x^{22}y^6$

4) $81x^{14}y^{10}$

5) $1,024x^{20}y^{30}$

6) $144x^2y^6$

7) $\frac{25}{x^2}$

8) x^6y^6

9) $\frac{25}{x^{10}}$

10) $\frac{x^4}{y^4}$

11) x^4y^2

12) $\frac{4y^8}{x^4}$

Zero and Negative Exponents

1) $\frac{1}{8}$

2) $\frac{1}{27}$

3) $\frac{1}{343}$

4) $\frac{1}{216}$

5) $\frac{1}{512}$

6) $\frac{1}{81}$

7) $\frac{1}{1,000}$

8) $\frac{1}{1,000,000,000}$

9) 2

10) 4

11) 9

12) $\frac{9}{4}$

Day 15: Exponents and Roots

Math Topics that you'll learn today:

- ✓ Negative Exponents and Negative Bases

- ✓ Scientific Notation

Mathematics is an independent world created out of pure intelligence.

~ William Woods Worth

Negative Exponents and Negative Bases

Step-by-step guide:

✓ Make the power positive. A negative exponent is the reciprocal of that number with a positive exponent.
✓ The parenthesis is important!
✓ 5^{-2} is not the same as $(-5)^{-2}$

$$(-5)^{-2} = -\frac{1}{5^2} \text{ and } (-5)^{-2} = +\frac{1}{5^2}$$

Example:

1) Simplify. $\left(\frac{3a}{2c}\right)^{-2} =$

Use Exponent's rules: $\frac{1}{x^b} = x^{-b} \to \left(\frac{3a}{2c}\right)^{-2} = \frac{1}{\left(\frac{3a}{2c}\right)^2} = \frac{1}{\frac{3^2 a^2}{2^2 c^2}}$

Now use fraction rule: $\frac{1}{\frac{b}{c}} = \frac{c}{b} \to \frac{1}{\frac{3^2 a^2}{2^2 c^2}} = \frac{2^2 c^2}{3^2 a^2}$

Then: $\frac{2^2 c^2}{3^2 a^2} = \frac{4c^2}{9a^2}$

2) Simplify. $\left(-\frac{5x}{3yz}\right)^{-3} =$

Use Exponent's rules: $\frac{1}{x^b} = x^{-b} \to \left(-\frac{5x}{3yz}\right)^{-3} = \frac{1}{\left(-\frac{5x}{3yz}\right)^3} = \frac{1}{-\frac{5^3 x^3}{3^3 y^3 z^3}}$

Now use fraction rule: $\frac{1}{\frac{b}{c}} = \frac{c}{b} \to \frac{1}{-\frac{5^3 x^3}{3^3 y^3 z^3}} = -\frac{3^3 y^3 z^3}{5^3 x^3} = -\frac{27 y^3 z^3}{125 x^3}$

✍ **Simplify.**

1) $-5x^{-2}y^{-3} =$

2) $20x^{-4}y^{-1} =$

3) $14a^{-6}b^{-7} =$

4) $-12x^2 y^{-3} =$

5) $-\frac{25}{x^{-6}} =$

6) $\frac{7b}{-9c^{-4}} =$

7) $\frac{7ab}{a^{-3}b^{-1}} =$

8) $-\frac{5n^{-2}}{10p^{-3}} =$

9) $\frac{4ab^{-2}}{-3c^{-2}} =$

10) $\left(\frac{3a}{2c}\right)^{-2} =$

11) $\left(-\frac{5x}{3yz}\right)^{-3} =$

12) $\frac{4ab^{-2}}{-3c^{-2}} =$

13) $\left(-\frac{x^3}{x^4}\right)^{-2} =$

Scientific Notation

Step-by-step guide:

- ✓ It is used to write very big or very small numbers in decimal form.
- ✓ In scientific notation all numbers are written in the form of:

$$m \times 10^n$$

Decimal notation	Scientific notation
5	5×10^0
$-25{,}000$	-2.5×10^4
0.5	5×10^{-1}
2,122.456	$2{,}122456 \times 10^3$

Example:

1) Write **0.00012** in scientific notation.

First, move the decimal point to the right so that you have a number that is between 1 and 10. Then: $N = 1.2$

Second, determine how many places the decimal moved in step 1 by the power of 10.

Then: 10^{-4} → When the decimal moved to the right, the exponent is negative.

Then: $0.00012 = 1.2 \times 10^{-4}$

2) Write **8.3×10^{-5}** in standard notation.

10^{-5} → When the decimal moved to the right, the exponent is negative.

Then: $8.3 \times 10^{-5} = 0.000083$

✎ *Write each number in scientific notation.*

1) $0.000325 =$ 3) $56{,}000{,}000 =$

2) $0.00023 =$ 4) $21{,}000 =$

✎ *Write each number in standard notation.*

5) $3 \times 10^{-1} =$ 7) $1.2 \times 10^3 =$

6) $5 \times 10^{-2} =$ 8) $2 \times 10^{-4} =$

Answers – Day 15

Negative Exponents and Negative Bases

1) $-\dfrac{5}{x^2 y^3}$

2) $\dfrac{20}{x^4 y}$

3) $\dfrac{14}{a^6 b^7}$

4) $-\dfrac{12x^2}{y^3}$

5) $-25x^6$

6) $-\dfrac{7bc^4}{9}$

7) $7a^4 b^2$

8) $-\dfrac{p^3}{2n^2}$

9) $-\dfrac{4ac^2}{3b^2}$

10) $\dfrac{4c^2}{9a^2}$

11) $-\dfrac{27y^3 z^3}{125x^3}$

12) $-\dfrac{4ac^2}{3b^2}$

13) x^2

Scientific Notation

1) 3.25×10^{-4}

2) 2.3×10^{-4}

3) 5.6×10^7

4) 2.1×10^4

5) 0.3

6) 0.05

7) 1,200

8) 0.0002

Day 16: Exponents and Roots

Math Topics that you'll learn today:

- ✓ Square Roots

- ✓ Simplifying Variable Expressions

"Life is a math equation. In order to gain the most, you have to know how to convert negatives into positives." -

Anonymous

Square Roots

Step-by-step guide:

    ✓ A square root of x is a number r whose square is: $r^2 = x$

               r is a square root of x.

Example:

1) Find the square root of $\sqrt{225}$.

    First factor the number: $225 = 15^2$, Then: $\sqrt{225} = \sqrt{15^2}$

    Now use radical rule: $\sqrt[n]{a^n} = a$

    Then: $\sqrt{15^2} = 15$

2) Evaluate. $\sqrt{4} \times \sqrt{16} =$

    First factor the numbers: $4 = 2^2$ and $16 = 4^2$

    Then: $\sqrt{4} \times \sqrt{16} = \sqrt{2^2} \times \sqrt{4^2}$

    Now use radical rule: $\sqrt[n]{a^n} = a$, Then: $\sqrt{2^2} \times \sqrt{4^2} = 2 \times 4 = 8$

✎ *Evaluate.*

1) $\sqrt{4} \times \sqrt{9} =$ _____

2) $\sqrt{25} \times \sqrt{64} =$ _____

3) $\sqrt{2} \times \sqrt{8} =$ _____

4) $\sqrt{6} \times \sqrt{6} =$ _____

5) $\sqrt{5} \times \sqrt{5} =$ _____

6) $\sqrt{8} \times \sqrt{8} =$ _____

7) $\sqrt{2} + \sqrt{2} =$ _____

8) $\sqrt{8} + \sqrt{8} =$ _____

9) $4\sqrt{5} - 2\sqrt{5} =$ _____

10) $3\sqrt{3} \times 2\sqrt{3} =$ _____

11) $8\sqrt{2} \times 2\sqrt{2} =$ _____

12) $6\sqrt{3} - \sqrt{12} =$ _____

Simplifying Variable Expressions

Step-by-step guide:

- ✓ In algebra, a variable is a letter used to stand for a number. The most common letters are: x, y, z, a, b, c, m, and n.
- ✓ algebraic expression is an expression contains integers, variables, and the math operations such as addition, subtraction, multiplication, division, etc.
- ✓ In an expression, we can combine "like" terms. (values with same variable and same power)

Examples:

1) Simplify this expression. $(\mathbf{10x + 2x + 3})$ =?
   Combine like terms. Then: $(10x + 2x + 3) = 12x + 3$ (remember you cannot combine variables and numbers.
2) Simplify this expression. $\mathbf{12 - 3x^2 + 9x + 5x^2}$ =?
   Combine "like" terms: $-3x^2 + 5x^2 = 2x^2$

   Then: $12 - 3x^2 + 9x + 5x^2 = 12 + 2x^2 + 9x$. Write in standard form (biggest powers first): $2x^2 + 9x + 12$

✎ *Simplify each expression.*

1) $(2x + x + 3 + 24) =$

2) $(-28x - 20x + 24) =$

3) $7x + 3 - 3x =$

4) $-2 - x^2 - 6x^2 =$

5) $3 + 10x^2 + 2 =$

6) $8x^2 + 6x + 7x^2 =$

7) $5x^2 - 12x^2 + 8x =$

8) $2x^2 - 2x - x =$

9) $4x + (12 - 30x) =$

10) $10x + (80x - 48) =$

11) $(-18x - 54) - 5 =$

12) $2x^2 + (-8x) =$

Answers – Day 16

Square Roots

1) 6

2) 40

3) 4

4) 6

5) 5

6) 8

7) $2\sqrt{2}$

8) $2\sqrt{8}$

9) $2\sqrt{5}$

10) 18

11) 32

12) $4\sqrt{3}$

Simplifying Variable Expressions

1) $3x + 27$

2) $-48x + 24$

3) $4x + 3$

4) $-7x^2 - 2$

5) $10x^2 + 5$

6) $15x^2 + 6x$

7) $-7x^2 + 8x$

8) $2x^2 - 3x$

9) $-26x + 12$

10) $90x - 48$

11) $-18x - 59$

12) $2x^2 - 8x$

Day 17: Expressions and Variables

Math Topics that you'll learn today:

- ✓ Simplifying Polynomial Expressions

- ✓ Translate Phrases into an Algebraic Statement

Simplifying Polynomial Expressions

Step-by-step guide:

✓ In mathematics, a polynomial is an expression consisting of variables and coefficients that involves only the operations of addition, subtraction, multiplication, and non-negative integer exponents of variables.

$$P(x) = a_n x^n + a_{n-1} x^{n-1} + \ldots + a_2 x^2 + a_1 x + a_0$$

Examples:

1) Simplify this Polynomial Expressions. $4x^2 - 5x^3 + 15x^4 - 12x^3 =$
   Combine "like" terms: $-5x^3 - 12x^3 = -17x^3$
   Then: $4x^2 - 5x^3 + 15x^4 - 12x^3 = 4x^2 - 17x^3 + 15x^4$
   Then write in standard form: $4x^2 - 17x^3 + 15x^4 = 15x^4 - 17x^3 + 4x^2$

2) Simplify this expression. $(2x^2 - x^4) - (4x^4 - x^2) =$
   First use distributive property: → multiply $(-)$ into $(4x^4 - x^2)$
   $(2x^2 - x^4) - (4x^4 - x^2) = 2x^2 - x^4 - 4x^4 + x^2$
   Then combine "like" terms: $2x^2 - x^4 - 4x^4 + x^2 = 3x^2 - 5x^4$
   And write in standard form: $3x^2 - 5x^4 = -5x^4 + 3x^2$

✎ *Simplify each polynomial.*

1) $(2x^3 + 5x^2) - (12x + 2x^2) =$ _____

2) $(2x^5 + 2x^3) - (7x^3 + 6x^2) =$ _____

3) $(12x^4 + 4x^2) - (2x^2 - 6x^4) =$ _____

4) $14x - 3x^2 - 2(6x^2 + 6x^3) =$ _____

5) $(5x^3 - 3) + 5(2x^2 - 3x^3) =$ _____

6) $(4x^3 - 2x) - 2(4x^3 - 2x^4) =$ _____

7) $2(4x - 3x^3) - 3(3x^3 + 4x^2) =$ _____

8) $(2x^2 - 2x) - (2x^3 + 5x^2) =$ _____

Translate Phrases into an Algebraic Statement

Step-by-step guide:

Translating key words and phrases into algebraic expressions:

- ✓ Addition: plus, more than, the sum of, etc.
- ✓ Subtraction: minus, less than, decreased, etc.
- ✓ Multiplication: times, product, multiplied, etc.
- ✓ Division: quotient, divided, ratio, etc.

Examples:

Write an algebraic expression for each phrase.

1) Eight more than a number is **20**.
   More than mean plus a number $= x$
   Then: $8 + x = 20$

2) 5 times the sum of **8** and x.
   Sum of 8 and x: $8 + x$. Times means multiplication. Then: $5 \times (8 + x)$

✎ *Write an algebraic expression for each phrase.*

1) 4 multiplied by x. _____

2) Subtract 8 from y. _____

3) 6 divided by x. _____

4) 12 decreased by y. _____

5) Add y to 9. _____

6) The square of 5. _____

7) x raised to the fourth power. _____

8) The sum of nine and a number. _____

9) The difference between sixty–four and y. _____

10) The quotient of twelve and a number. _____

11) The quotient of the square of x and 7. _____

12) The difference between x and 8 is 22. _____

Answers – Day 17

Simplifying Polynomial Expressions

1) $2x^3 + 3x^2 - 12x$

2) $2x^5 - 5x^3 - 6x^2$

3) $18x^4 + 2x^2$

4) $-12x^3 - 15x^2 + 14x$

5) $-10x^3 + 10x^2 - 3$

6) $4x^4 - 4x^3 - 2$

7) $-15x^3 - 12x^2 + 8x$

8) $-2x^3 - 3x^2 - 2x$

Translate Phrases into an Algebraic Statement

1) $4x$

2) $y - 8$

3) $\frac{6}{x}$

4) $12 - y$

5) $y + 9$

6) 5^2

7) x^4

8) $9 + x$

9) $64 - y$

10) $\frac{12}{x}$

11) $\frac{x^2}{7}$

12) $x - 8 = 22$

Day 18: Evaluating Variables

Math Topics that you'll learn today:

- ✓ The Distributive Property

- ✓ Evaluating One Variable

Mathematics is on the artistic side a creation of new rhythms, orders, designs, harmonies, and on the knowledge side, is a systematic study of various rhythms, orders. – William L. Schaaf

The Distributive Property

Step-by-step guide:

✓ Distributive Property:
$$a(b + c) = ab + ac$$

Examples:

1) Simply. $(5x - 3)(-5) =$

Use Distributive Property formula: $a(b + c) = ab + ac$
$(5x - 3)(-5) = -25x + 15$

2) Simply. $(-8)(2x - 8) =$

Use Distributive Property formula: $a(b + c) = ab + ac$
$(-8)(2x - 8) = -16x + 64$

✎ *Use the distributive property to simply each expression.*

1) $2(2 + 3x) =$

2) $3(5 + 5x) =$

3) $4(3x - 8) =$

4) $(6x - 2)(-2) =$

5) $(-3)(x + 2) =$

6) $(2 + 2x)5 =$

7) $(-4)(4 - 2x) =$

8) $-(-2 - 5x) =$

9) $(-6x + 2)(-1) =$

10) $(-5)(x - 2) =$

11) $-(7 - 3x) =$

12) $8(8 + 2x) =$

Evaluating One Variable

Step-by-step guide:

- ✓ To evaluate one variable expression, find the variable and substitute a number for that variable.
- ✓ Perform the arithmetic operations.

Examples:

1) Solve this expression. $12 - 2x, x = -1$

First substitute -1 for x, then:

$12 - 2x = 12 - 2(-1) = 12 + 2 = 14$

2) Solve this expression. $-8 + 5x, x = 3$

First substitute 3 for x, then:

$-8 + 5x = -8 + 5(3) = -8 + 15 = 7$

✍ *Evaluate each expression using the value given.*

1) $5 + x, x = 2$

2) $x - 2, x = 4$

3) $8x + 1, x = 9$

4) $x - 12, x = -1$

5) $9 - x, x = 3$

6) $x + 2, x = 5$

7) $3x + 7, x = 6$

8) $x + (-5), x = -2$

9) $3x + 6, x = 4$

10) $4x + 6, x = -1$

11) $10 + 2x - 6, x = 3$

12) $10 - 3x, x = 8$

Answers – Day 18

The Distributive Property

1) $6x + 4$

2) $15x + 15$

3) $12x - 32$

4) $-12x + 4$

5) $-3x - 6$

6) $10x + 10$

7) $8x - 16$

8) $5x + 2$

9) $6x - 2$

10) $-5x + 10$

11) $3x - 7$

12) $16x + 64$

Evaluating One Variable

1) 7

2) 2

3) 73

4) -13

5) 6

6) 7

7) 25

8) -7

9) 18

10) 2

11) 10

12) -14

Day 19: Evaluating Variables

Math Topics that you'll learn today:

- ✓ Evaluating Two Variables

- ✓ Combining like Terms

Mathematics is, as it were, a sensuous logic, and relates to philosophy as do the arts, music, and plastic art to poetry.

~ K. Shegel

Evaluating Two Variables

Step-by-step guide:

✓ To evaluate an algebraic expression, substitute a number for each variable and perform the arithmetic operations.

Examples:

1) Solve this expression. $-3x + 5y, x = 2, y = -1$

First substitute 2 for x, and -1 for y, then:

$-3x + 5y = -3(2) + 5(-1) = -6 - 5 = -11$

2) Solve this expression. $2(a - 2b), a = -1, b = 3$

First substitute -1 for a, and 3 for b, then:

$2(a - 2b) = 2a - 4b = 2(-1) - 4(3) = -2 - 12 = -14$

✎ *Evaluate each expression using the values given.*

1) $2x + 4y,$

   $x = 3, y = 2$

2) $8x + 5y,$

   $x = 1, y = 5$

3) $-2a + 4b,$

   $a = 6, b = 3$

4) $4x + 7 - 2y,$

   $x = 7, y = 6$

5) $5z + 12 - 4k,$

   $z = 5, k = 2$

6) $2(-x - 2y),$

   $x = 6, y = 9$

7) $18a + 2b,$

   $a = 2, b = 8$

8) $4x \div 3y,$

   $x = 3, y = 2$

9) $2x + 15 + 4y,$

   $x = -2, y = 4$

10) $4a - (15 - b),$

   $a = 4, b = 6$

11) $5z + 19 + 8k,$

   $z = -5, k = 4$

12) $xy + 12 + 5x,$

   $x = 7, y = 2$

Combining like Terms

Step-by-step guide:

✓ Terms are separated by "+" and "–" signs.
✓ Like terms are terms with same variables and same powers.
✓ Be sure to use the "+" or "–" that is in front of the coefficient.

Examples:

1) Simplify this expression. $(-5)(8x - 6) =$

Use Distributive Property formula: $a(b + c) = a + ac$
$(-5)(8x - 6) = -40x + 30$

2) Simplify this expression. $(-3)(2x - 2) + 6 =$

First use Distributive Property formula: $a(b + c) = ab + ac$
$(-3)(2x - 2) + 6 = -6x + 6 + 6$

And Combining like Terms:

$-6x + 6 + 6 = -6x + 12$

✎ *Simplify each expression.*

1) $2x + x + 2 =$

2) $2(5x - 3) =$

3) $7x - 2x + 8 =$

4) $(-4)(3x - 5) =$

5) $9x - 7x - 5 =$

6) $16x - 5 + 8x =$

7) $5 - (5x + 6) =$

8) $-12x + 7 - 10x =$

9) $7x - 11 - 2x + 2 =$

10) $12x + 4x - 21 =$

11) $5 + 2x - 8 =$

12) $(-2x + 6)^2 =$

Answers – Day 19

Evaluating Two Variables

1) 14

2) 33

3) 0

4) 23

5) 29

6) -48

7) 52

8) 2

9) 27

10) 7

11) 26

12) 61

Combining like Terms

1) $3x + 2$

2) $10x - 6$

3) $5x + 8$

4) $-12x + 20$

5) $2x - 5$

6) $24x - 5$

7) $-5x - 1$

8) $-22x + 7$

9) $5x - 9$

10) $16x - 21$

11) $2x - 3$

12) $4x^2 - 24x + 36$

Day 20: Equations and Inequalities

Math Topics that you'll learn today:

- ✓ One–Step Equations

- ✓ Multi–Step Equations

- ✓ Graphing Single–Variable Inequalities

"Life is a math equation. In order to gain the most, you have to know how to convert negatives into positives."

- Anonymous

One–Step Equations

Step-by-step guide:

✓ The values of two expressions on both sides of an equation are equal. $ax + b = c$

✓ You only need to perform one Math operation in order to solve the one-step equations.

✓ To solve one-step equation, find the inverse (opposite) operation is being performed.

✓ The inverse operations are:

  - Addition and subtraction
  - Multiplication and division

Examples:

1) Solve this equation. $x + 24 = 0$, $x = ?$

   Here, the operation is addition and its inverse operation is subtraction. To solve this equation, subtract 24 from both sides of the equation: $x + 24 - 24 = 0 - 24$

   Then simplify: $x + 24 - 24 = 0 - 24 \rightarrow x = -24$

2) Solve this equation. $3x = 15$, $x = ?$

   Here, the operation is multiplication (variable x is multiplied by 3) and its inverse operation is division. To solve this equation, divide both sides of equation by 3:

   $$3x = 15 \rightarrow 3x \div 3 = 15 \div 3 \rightarrow x = 5$$

✎ Solve each equation.

1) $16 = -4 + x, x =$ ____

2) $x - 4 = -25, x =$ ____

3) $x + 12 = -9, x =$ ____

4) $14 = 18 - x, x =$ ____

5) $2 + x = -14, x =$ ____

6) $x - 5 = 15, x =$ ____

7) $25 = x - 5, x =$ ____

8) $x - 3 = -12, x =$ ____

9) $x - 12 = 12, x =$ ____

10) $x - 12 = -25, x =$ ____

11) $x - 13 = 32, x =$ ____

12) $-55 = x - 18, x =$ ____

Multi–Step Equations

Step-by-step guide:

- ✓ Combine "like" terms on one side.
- ✓ Bring variables to one side by adding or subtracting.
- ✓ Simplify using the inverse of addition or subtraction.
- ✓ Simplify further by using the inverse of multiplication or division.

Examples:

1) Solve this equation. $-(2 - x) = 5$

First use Distributive Property: $-(2 - x) = -2 + x$

Now solve by adding 2 to both sides of the equation. $-2 + x = 5 \rightarrow -2 + x + 2 = 5 + 2$

Now simplify: $-2 + x + 2 = 5 + 2 \rightarrow x = 7$

2) Solve this equation. $4x + 10 = 25 - x$

First bring variables to one side by adding x to both sides.

$4x + 10 + x = 25 - x + x \rightarrow 5x + 10 = 25$. Now, subtract 10 from both sides:

$5x + 10 - 10 = 25 - 10 \rightarrow 5x = 15$

Now, divide both sides by 5: $5x = 15 \rightarrow 5x \div 5 = \frac{15}{5} \rightarrow x = 3$

✎ *Solve each equation.*

1) $-3(2 + x) = 3$

2) $-2(4 + x) = 4$

3) $20 = -(x - 8)$

4) $2(2 - 2x) = 20$

5) $-12 = -(2x + 8)$

6) $5(2 + x) = 5$

7) $2(x - 14) = 4$

8) $-28 = 2x + 12x$

9) $3x + 15 = -x - 5$

10) $2(3 + 2x) = -18$

11) $12 - 2x = -8 - x$

12) $10 - 3x = 14 + x$

Graphing Single–Variable Inequalities

Step-by-step guide:

- ✓ Inequality is similar to equations and uses symbols for "less than" (<) and "greater than" (>).
- ✓ To solve inequalities, we need to isolate the variable. (like in equations)
- ✓ To graph an inequality, find the value of the inequality on the number line.
- ✓ For less than or greater than draw open circle on the value of the variable.
- ✓ If there is an equal sign too, then use filled circle.
- ✓ Draw a line to the right or to the left for greater or less than.

Examples:

1) Draw a graph for $x > 2$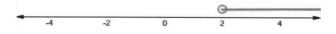

Since, the variable is greater than 2, then we need to find 2 and draw an open circle above it. Then, draw a line to the right.

Graph this inequality. $x < 5$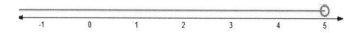

✎ **Draw a graph for each inequality.**

1) $x > -1$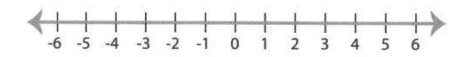

2) $x < 3$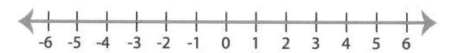

3) $x < -5$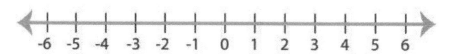

4) $x > -2$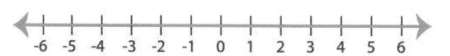

5) $x < 0$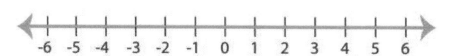

Answers – Day 20

One–Step Equations

1) 20

2) −21

3) −21

4) 4

5) −16

6) 20

7) 30

8) −9

9) 24

10) −13

11) 45

12) −37

Multi–Step Equations

1) −3

2) −6

3) −12

4) −4

5) 2

6) −1

7) 16

8) −2

9) −5

10) −6

11) 20

12) −1

Graphing Single–Variable Inequalities

1)

2)

3)

4)

5)

Day 21: Solving Inequalities

Math Topics that you'll learn today:

- ✓ One–Step Inequalities

- ✓ Multi–Step Inequalities

Without mathematics, there's nothing you can do. Everything around you is mathematics. Everything around you is numbers." ~ Shakuntala Devi

One–Step Inequalities

Step-by-step guide:

- ✓ Similar to equations, first isolate the variable by using inverse operation.
- ✓ For dividing or multiplying both sides by negative numbers, flip the direction of the inequality sign.

Examples:

1) Solve and graph the inequality. $x + 2 \geq 3$.

Subtract 2 from both sides. $x + 2 \geq 3 \rightarrow x + 2 - 2 \geq 3 - 2$, then: $x \geq 1$

2) Solve this inequality. $x - 1 \leq 2$

Add 1 to both sides. $x - 1 \leq 2 \rightarrow x - 1 + 1 \leq 2 + 1$, then: $x \leq 3$

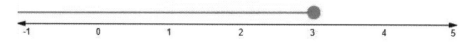

✐ Solve each inequality and graph it.

1) $2x \geq 12$

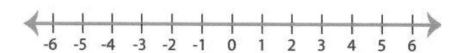

2) $4 + x \leq 5$

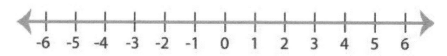

3) $x + 3 \leq -3$

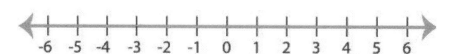

4) $4x \geq 16$

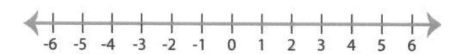

5) $9x \leq 18$

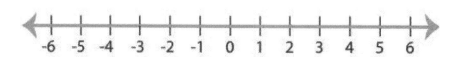

Multi–Step Inequalities

Step-by-step guide:

- ✓ Isolate the variable.
- ✓ Simplify using the inverse of addition or subtraction.
- ✓ Simplify further by using the inverse of multiplication or division.

Examples:

1) Solve this inequality. $2x - 2 \leq 6$

First add 2 to both sides: $2x - 2 + 2 \leq 6 + 2 \rightarrow 2x \leq 8$

Now, divide both sides by 2: $2x \leq 8 \rightarrow x \leq 4$

2) Solve this inequality. $2x - 4 \leq 8$

First add 4 to both sides: $2x - 4 + 4 \leq 8 + 4$

Then simplify: $2x - 4 + 4 \leq 8 + 4 \rightarrow 2x \leq 12$

Now divide both sides by 2: $\frac{2x}{2} \leq \frac{12}{2} \rightarrow x \leq 6$

✍ *Solve each inequality.*

1) $2x - 8 \leq 6$

2) $8x - 2 \leq 14$

3) $-5 + 3x \leq 10$

4) $2(x - 3) \leq 6$

5) $7x - 5 \leq 9$

6) $4x - 21 < 19$

7) $2x - 3 < 21$

8) $17 - 3x \geq -13$

9) $9 + 4x < 21$

10) $3 + 2x \geq 19$

11) $6 + 2x < 32$

12) $4x - 1 < 7$

Answers – Day 21

One–Step Inequalities

1)
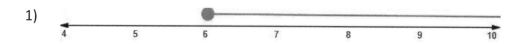

2)

3)

4)
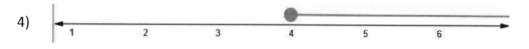

5)

Multi–Step inequalities

1) $x \leq 7$
2) $x \leq 2$
3) $x \leq 5$
4) $x \leq 6$
5) $x \leq 2$
6) $x < 10$

7) $x < 12$
8) $x \leq 10$
9) $x < 3$
10) $x \geq 8$
11) $x < 13$
12) $x < 2$

Day 22: Triangles

Math Topics that you'll learn today:

- ✓ The Pythagorean Theorem

- ✓ Triangles

The Pythagorean Theorem

Step-by-step guide:

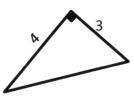

✓ In any right triangle: $a^2 + b^2 = c^2$

Example:

1) Find the missing length.

Use Pythagorean Theorem: $a^2 + b^2 = c^2$

Then: $a^2 + b^2 = c^2 \rightarrow 3^2 + 4^2 = c^2 \rightarrow 9 + 16 = c^2$

$c^2 = 25 \rightarrow c = 5$

2) Right triangle ABC has two legs of lengths **6 cm** (AB) and **8 cm** (AC). What is the length of the third side (BC)?

Use Pythagorean Theorem: $a^2 + b^2 = c^2$

Then: $a^2 + b^2 = c^2 \rightarrow 6^2 + 8^2 = c^2 \rightarrow 36 + 64 = c^2$

$c^2 = 100 \rightarrow c = 10$

✍ ***Find the missing side.***

1)	2)	3)	4)

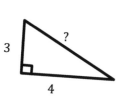

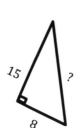

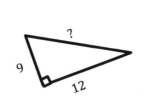

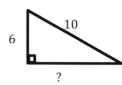

5)	6)	7)	8)

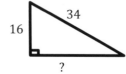

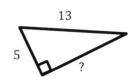

Triangles

Step-by-step guide:

✓ In any triangle the sum of all angles is **180** degrees.
✓ Area of a triangle $= \frac{1}{2}\,(base \times height)$

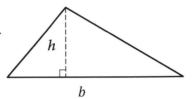

Example:

What is the area of triangles?

1)

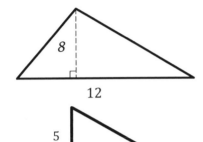

Solution:

Use the are formula: Area $= \frac{1}{2}\,(base \times height)$

$base = 12$ and $height = 8$

Area $= \frac{1}{2}(12 \times 8) = \frac{1}{2}(96) = 48$

2)

Solution:

Use the are formula: Area $= \frac{1}{2}\,(base \times height)$

$base = 6$ and $height = 5$

Area $= \frac{1}{2}(5 \times 6) = \frac{30}{2} = 15$

✎ *Find the measure of the unknown angle in each triangle.*

1)

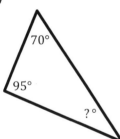

2)

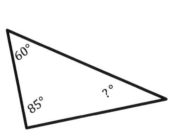

3)

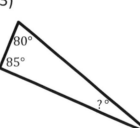

4)

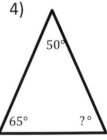

✎ *Find area of each triangle.*

5)

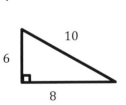

6)

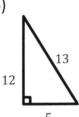

7)

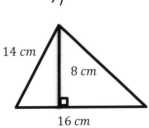

8)

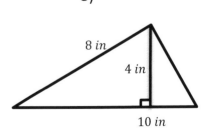

Answers – Day 22

The Pythagorean Theorem

1) 5

2) 17

3) 15

4) 8

5) 5

6) 30

7) 30

8) 12

Triangles

1) 15°

2) 35°

3) 15°

4) 65°

5) 24 square unites

6) 30 square unites

7) 64 square unites

8) 20 square unites

Day 23: Polygons and Circles

Math Topics that you'll learn today:

- ✓ Polygons

- ✓ Circles

"If people do not believe that mathematics is simple, it is only because they do not realize how complicated life is."

— *John von Neumann*

Polygons

Step-by-step guide:

Perimeter of a square $= 4 \times side = 4s$ s	Perimeter of a rectangle $= 2(width + length)$ 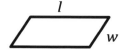 width length
Perimeter of trapezoid $= a + b + c + d$ 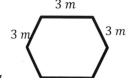	Perimeter of a regular hexagon $= 6a$ 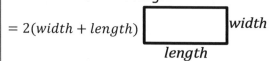 a

Example: Find the perimeter of following regular hexagon.

Perimeter of Pentagon $= 6a$

Perimeter of Pentagon $= 6a = 6 \times 3 = 18m$

Perimeter of a parallelogram $= 2(l + w)$

Find the perimeter of each shape.

1)
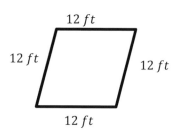
12 ft
12 ft
12 ft
12 ft

2)
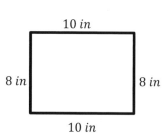
10 in
8 in   8 in
10 in

3)
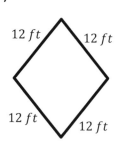
12 ft   12 ft
12 ft   12 ft

4) Square
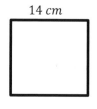
14 cm

5) Regular hexagon
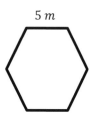
5 m

6)
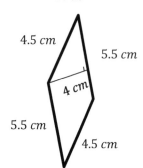
4.5 cm
5.5 cm
4 cm
5.5 cm
4.5 cm

7) Parallelogram
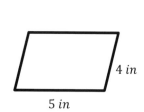
4 in
5 in

8) Square

6 m

Circles

Step-by-step guide:

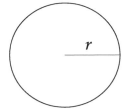

- ✓ In a circle, variable r is usually used for the radius and d for diameter and π is about 3.14.
- ✓ Area of a circle $= \pi r^2$
- ✓ Circumference of a circle $= 2\pi r$

Example:

1) Find the area of the circle.

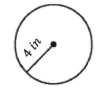

Use area formula: $Area = \pi r^2$,

$r = 4$ then: $Area = \pi(4)^2 = 16\pi$, $\pi = 3.14$ then: $Area = 16 \times 3.14 = 50.24$

2) Find the Circumference of the circle.

Use Circumference formula: $Circumference = 2\pi r$

$r = 6$, then: $Circumference = 2\pi(6) = 12\pi$

$\pi = 3.14$ then: $Circumference = 12 \times 3.14 = 37.68$

✏️ ***Complete the table below.*** $(\pi = 3.14)$

	Radius	Diameter	Circumference	Area
Circle 1	4 inches	8 inches	25.12 inches	50.24 square inches
Circle 2		12 meters		
Circle 3				12.56 square ft
Circle 4			18.84 miles	
Circle 5		5 kilometers		
Circle 6	6 centimeters			
Circle 7		8 feet		
Circle 8				28.26 square meters

Answers – Day 23

Polygons

1) 48 *ft*
2) 36 *in*
3) 48 *ft*
4) 56 *cm*
5) 30 *m*
6) 20 *cm*
7) 18 *in*
8) 24 *m*

Circles

	Radius	Diameter	Circumference	Area
Circle 1	4 *inches*	8 *inches*	25.12 *inches*	50.24 *square inches*
Circle 2	6 *meters*	12 *meters*	37.68 *meters*	113.04 *meters*
Circle 3	2 *square ft*	4 *square ft*	12.56 *square ft*	12.56 *square ft*
Circle 4	3 *miles*	6 *miles*	18.84 *miles*	28.26 *miles*
Circle 5	2.5 *kilometers*	5 *kilometers*	15.7 *kilometers*	19.625 *kilometers*
Circle 6	6 *centimeters*	12 *centimeters*	37.68 *centimeters*	113.04 *centimeters*
Circle 7	4 *feet*	8 *feet*	25.12 *feet*	50.24 *feet*
Circle 8	3 *square meters*	6 *square meters*	18.84 *square meters*	28.26 *square meters*

Day 24: Trapezoids and Cubes

Math Topics that you'll learn today:

- ✓ Trapezoids

- ✓ Cubes

Trapezoids

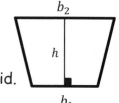

Step-by-step guide:

  ✓ A quadrilateral with at least one pair of parallel sides is a trapezoid.
  ✓ Area of a trapezoid = $\frac{1}{2}h(b_1 + b_2)$

Example:

Calculate the area of the trapezoid.

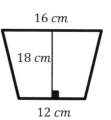

  Use area formula: $A = \frac{1}{2}h(b_1 + b_2)$

  $b_1 = 12$, $b_2 = 16$ and $h = 18$

  Then: $A = \frac{1}{2}18(12 + 16) = 9(28) = 252\ cm^2$

✏️ **Find the area of each trapezoid.**

1)	2)	3)	4)
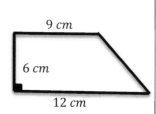	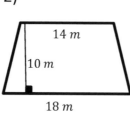	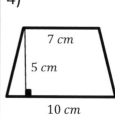	

5)	6)	7)	8)
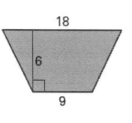	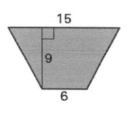	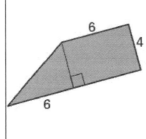	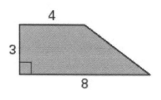

Cubes

Step-by-step guide:

- ✓ A cube is a three-dimensional solid object bounded by six square sides.
- ✓ Volume is the measure of the amount of space inside of a solid figure, like a cube, ball, cylinder or pyramid.
- ✓ Volume of a cube $= (one\ side)^3$
- ✓ surface area of cube $= 6 \times (one\ side)^2$

Example:

Find the volume and surface area of this cube.

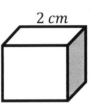
2 cm

Use volume formula: $volume = (one\ side)^3$

Then: $volume = (one\ side)^3 = (2)^3 = 8\ cm^3$

Use surface area formula:

$surface\ area\ of\ cube$: $6(one\ side)^2 = 6(2)^2 = 6(4) = 24\ cm^2$

✍ *Find the volume of each cube.*

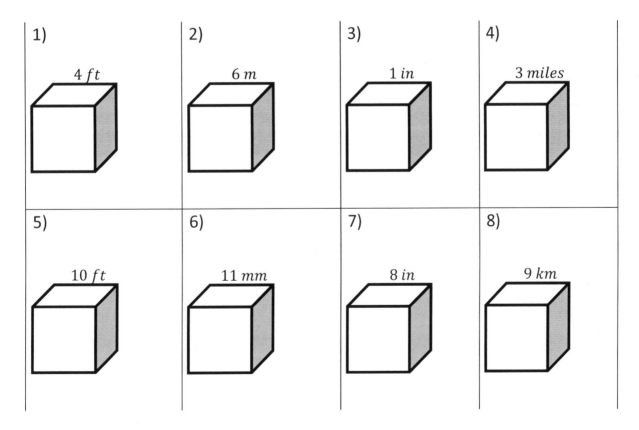

1) 4 ft

2) 6 m

3) 1 in

4) 3 miles

5) 10 ft

6) 11 mm

7) 8 in

8) 9 km

Answers – Day 24

Trapezoids

1) $63 \ cm^2$

2) $160 \ m^2$

3) $24 \ ft^2$

4) $42.5 \ cm^2$

5) 81

6) 94.5

7) 36

8) 18

Cubes

1) $64 \ ft^3$

2) $216 \ m^3$

3) $1 \ in^3$

4) $27 \ miles^3$

5) $1,000 \ ft^3$

6) $1,331 \ mm^3$

7) $512 \ in^3$

8) $729 \ km^3$

Day 25: Rectangular Prisms and Cylinder

Math Topics that you'll learn today:

- ✓ Rectangle Prisms

- ✓ Cylinder

It's fine to work on any problem, so long as it generates interesting mathematics along the way – even if you don't solve it at the end of the day." – Andrew Wiles

Rectangular Prisms

Step-by-step guide:

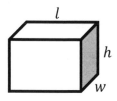

✓ A solid 3-dimensional object which has six rectangular faces.
✓ Volume of a Rectangular prism = **Length × Width × Height**

Volume = $l \times w \times h$ Surface area = $2(wh + lw + lh)$

Example:

Find the volume and surface area of rectangular prism.

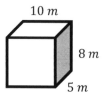

Use volume formula: $Volume = l \times w \times h$

Then: $Volume = 10 \times 5 \times 8 = 400 \ m^3$

Use surface area formula: $Surface \ area = 2(wh + lw + lh)$

Then: $Surface \ area = 2(5 \times 8 + 10 \times 5 + 10 \times 8) = 2(40 + 50 + 80) = 340 \ m^2$

✏ *Find the volume of each Rectangular Prism.*

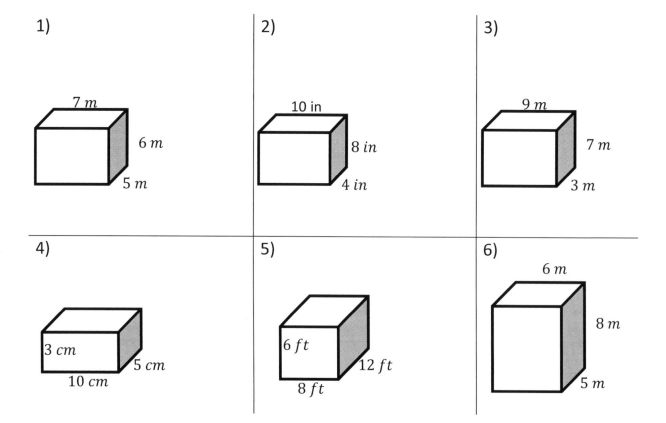

1)

7 m   6 m   5 m

2)

10 in   8 in   4 in

3)

9 m   7 m   3 m

4)

3 cm   5 cm   10 cm

5)

6 ft   12 ft   8 ft

6)

6 m   8 m   5 m

Cylinder

Step-by-step guide:

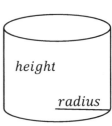

✓ A cylinder is a solid geometric figure with straight parallel sides and a circular or oval cross section.
✓ *Volume of Cylinder Formula* $= \pi(radius)^2 \times height \quad \pi = 3.14$
✓ *Surface area of a cylinder* $= 2\pi r^2 + 2\pi rh$

Example:

Find the volume and Surface area of the follow Cylinder.

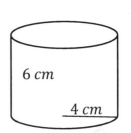

Use volume formula: $Volume = \pi(radius)^2 \times height$
Then: $Volume = \pi(4)^2 \times 6 = \pi 16 \times 6 = 96\pi$
$\pi = 3.14$ then: $Volume = 96\pi = 301.44$
Use surface area formula: $Surface\ area = 2\pi r^2 + 2\pi rh$
Then: $= 2\pi(4)^2 + 2\pi(4)(6) = 2\pi(16) + 2\pi(24) = 32\pi + 48\pi = 80\pi$
$\pi = 3.14$ then: $Surface\ area = 80 \times 3.14 = 251.2$

✍️ *Find the volume of each Cylinder. Round your answer to the nearest tenth.* $(\pi = 3.14)$

1)

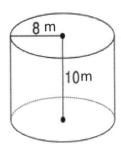

8 m

10m

2)

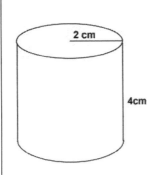

2 cm

4cm

3)

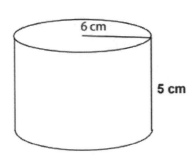

6 cm

5 cm

4)

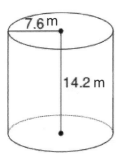

7.6 m

14.2 m

5)

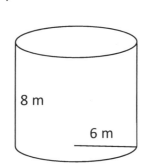

8 m

6 m

6)

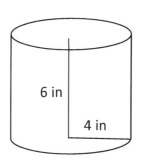

6 in

4 in

Answers – Day 25

Rectangle Prisms

1) $210\ m^3$

2) $320\ in^3$

3) $189\ m^3$

4) $150\ cm^3$

5) $576\ ft^3$

6) $240\ m^3$

Cylinder

1) $2,009.6\ m^3$

2) $50.24\ cm^3$

3) $565.2\ cm^3$

4) $2,575.4\ m^3$

5) $904.3\ m^3$

6) $301.4\ in^3$

Day 26: Statistics

Math Topics that you'll learn today:

- ✓ Mean, Median, Mode, and Range of the Given Data

- ✓ Histograms

Mean, Median, Mode, and Range of the Given Data

Step-by-step guide:

- ✓ Mean: $\dfrac{\text{sum of the data}}{\text{total number of data entires}}$
- ✓ Mode: value in the list that appears most often
- ✓ Range: the difference of largest value and smallest value in the list

Example:

1) What is the median of these numbers? **4, 9, 13, 8, 15, 18, 5**

   Write the numbers in order: 4, 5, 8, 9, 13, 15, 18

   Median is the number in the middle. Therefore, the median is 9.

2) What is the mode of these numbers? **22, 16, 12, 9, 7, 6, 4, 6**

   Mode: value in the list that appears most often
   Therefore, mode is 6.

✍ Solve.

1) In a javelin throw competition, five athletics score 56, 58, 63, 57 and 61 meters. What are their Mean and Median? _____

2) Eva went to shop and bought 3 apples, 5 peaches, 8 bananas, 1 pineapple and 3 melons. What are the Mean and Median of her purchase? _____

✍ Find Mode and Rage of the Given Data.

3) 8, 2, 5, 9, 1, 2

Mode: _____   Range: _____

4) 4, 4, 3, 9, 7, 9, 4, 6, 4

Mode: _____   Range: _____

5) 6, 6, 2, 3, 6, 3, 9, 12

Mode: _____   Range: _____

6) 12, 9, 2, 9, 3, 2, 9, 5

Mode: _____   Range: _____

Histograms

Step-by-step guide:

- ✓ A histogram is an accurate representation of the distribution of numerical data.

Example:

Use the following Graph to complete the table.

Answer:

Day	Distance (km)
1	
2	

→

Day	Distance (km)
1	359
2	460
3	278
4	547
5	360

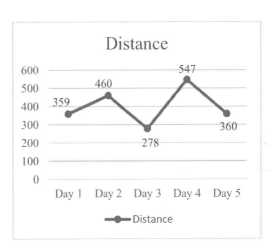

✍ The following table shows the number of births in the US from 2007 to 2012 (in millions).

Year	Number of births (in millions)
2007	4.32
2008	4.25
2009	4.13
2010	4
2011	3.95
2012	3.95

Draw a histogram for the table.

Answers – Day 26

Mean, Median, Mode, and Range of the Given Data

1) Mean: 59, Median: 58

2) Mean: 4, Median: 3

3) Mode: 2, Range: 8

4) Mode: 4, Range: 6

5) Mode: 6, Range: 10

6) Mode: 9, Range: 10

Histograms

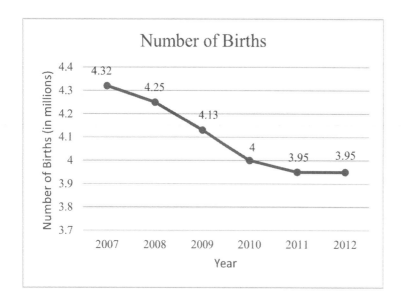

Day 27: Statistics and Probabilities

Math Topics that you'll learn today:

- ✓ Pie Graph

- ✓ Probability Problems

"A Man is like a fraction whose numerator is what he is and whose denominator is what he thinks of himself. The larger the denominator, the smaller the fraction." ~Tolstoy

Pie Graph

Step-by-step guide:

- ✓ A Pie Chart is a circle chart divided into sectors; each sector represents the relative size of each value.

Example:

A library has **840** books that include Mathematics, Physics, Chemistry, English and History. Use following graph to answer question.

What is the number of Mathematics books?

Number of total books $= 840$,
Percent of Mathematics books $= 30\% = 0.30$
Then: $0.30 \times 840 = 252$

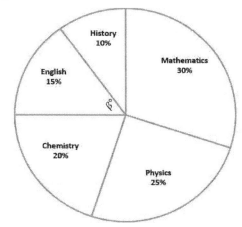

✍ **The circle graph below shows all Jason's expenses for last month. Jason spent $300 on his bills last month.**

1) How much did Jason spend on his car last month? _____

2) How much did Jason spend for foods last month? _____

3) How much did Jason spend on his rent last month? _____

4) What fraction is Jason's expenses for his bills and Car out of his total expenses last month?

Jason's monthly expenses

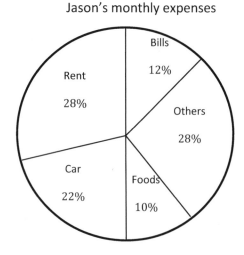

Probability Problems

Step-by-step guide:

- ✓ Probability is the likelihood of something happening in the future. It is expressed as a number between zero (can never happen) to **1** (will always happen).
- ✓ Probability can be expressed as a fraction, a decimal, or a percent.

Example:

1) If there are **8** red balls and **12** blue balls in a basket, what is the probability that John will pick out a red ball from the basket?

   There are 8 red ball and 20 are total number of balls. Therefore, probability that John will pick out a red ball from the basket is 8 out of 20 or $\frac{8}{8+12} = \frac{8}{20} = \frac{2}{5}$.

2) A bag contains **18** balls: two green, five black, eight blue, a brown, a red and one white. If **17** balls are removed from the bag at random, what is the probability that a brown ball has been removed?

   If 17 balls are removed from the bag at random, there will be one ball in the bag.

   The probability of choosing a brown ball is 1 out of 18. Therefore, the probability of not choosing a brown ball is 17 out of 18 and the probability of having not a brown ball after removing 17 balls is the same.

✎ *Solve.*

1) A number is chosen at random from **1** to **10**. Find the probability of selecting number **4** or smaller numbers. _____

2) Bag A contains 9 red marbles and 3 green marbles. Bag B contains 9 black marbles and 6 orange marbles. What is the probability of selecting a green marble at random from bag A? What is the probability of selecting a black marble at random from Bag B? _____

Answers – Day 27

Pie Graph

1) $550

2) $250

3) $700

4) $\frac{17}{50}$

Probability Problems

1) $\frac{2}{5}$

2) $\frac{1}{4}, \frac{3}{5}$

Day 28: Measurements

Math Topics that you'll learn today:

- ✓ Convert Measurement Units
- ✓ Distance Measurement
- ✓ Weight Measurement

Mathematics is no more computation than typing is literature.

- John Allen Paulos

Convert Measurement Units

Step-by-step guide:

✓ $1\ inch = 2.5\ cm$
✓ $1\ foot = 12\ inches$
✓ $1\ yard = 3\ feet$
✓ $1\ yard = 36\ inches$
✓ $1\ inch = 0.0254\ m$

Example:

1) Convert **10** inches to *cm*.

$1\ inch = 2.5\ cm$

Then: $10 \times 2.5 = 25$

2) Convert **144** inches to yard.

$1\ yard = 36\ inches$

Then: $\frac{144}{36} = 4$

✍ **Convert to an appropriate measurement unit. (Round to the nearest Hundredths)**

1) $4\ feet = $ ____ $inches$

2) $8\ inches = $ ____ $foot$

3) $10\ feet = $ ____ m

4) $15\ cm = $ ____ m

5) $5\ inches = $ ____ cm

6) $10\ inches = $ ____ m

7) $15\ inches = $ ____ cm

8) $12\ inches = $ ____ m

9) $8\ feet = $ ____ $inches$

10) $25\ cm = $ ____ $inches$

11) $11\ inches = $ ____ cm

12) $80\ inches = $ ____ m

Distance Measurement

Step-by-step guide:

✓ **1 mile = 5,280 ft**
✓ **1 mile = 1,760 yd**
✓ **1 mile = 1,609.34 m**

Example:

1) Convert **5** miles to **ft**.

$1\ mile = 5,280\ ft$

Then: $5 \times 5,280 = 26,400$

2) Convert **8** miles to yd.

$1\ miles = 1,760$

Then: $8 \times 1,760 = 14,080$

✎ **Convert to the new units. (Round to the nearest Hundredths)**

1) $10\ mi = $ _____ yd

2) $9\ mi = $ _____ yd

3) $12\ mi = $ _____ yd

4) $10\ mi = $ _____ ft

5) $15\ mi = $ _____ ft

6) $20\ mi = $ _____ yd

7) $16\ mi = $ _____ yd

8) $2\ mi = $ _____ ft

9) $21\ mi = $ _____ ft

10) $6\ mi = $ _____ ft

11) $3\ mi = $ _____ yd

12) $72\ mi = $ _____ ft

Weight Measurement

Step-by-step guide:

    ✓ $1\,kg = 1,000g$

Example:

1) Convert **500** gram to *kg*.

    $1\,kg = 1,000\,g$

    Then: $\dfrac{500}{1,000} = 0.5$

2) Convert **6** kg to *g*.

    $1\,kg = 1,000\,g$

    Then: $6 \times 1,000 = 6,000$

✍ *Convert to grams.*

1) $0.01\,kg =$ _____ g 4) $0.05\,kg =$ _____ g

2) $0.2\,kg =$ _____ g 5) $0.5\,kg =$ _____ g

3) $0.04\,kg =$ _____ g 6) $3.2\,kg =$ _____ g

✍ *Convert to kilograms.*

7) $20,000\,g =$ _____ kg 10) $150,000\,g =$ _____ kg

8) $3,000\,g =$ _____ kg 11) $120,000\,g =$ _____ kg

9) $100,000\,g =$ _____ kg 12) $200,000\,g =$ _____ kg

Answers – Day 28

Convert Measurement Units

1) $4\ feet = 48\ inches$

2) $8\ inches = 0.67\ foot$

3) $10\ feet = 3.05\ m$

4) $15\ cm = 0.15\ m$

5) $5\ inches = 12.7\ cm$

6) $10\ inches = 0.25\ m$

7) $15\ inches = 38.1\ cm$

8) $12\ inches = 0.3\ m$

9) $8\ feet = 96\ inches$

10) $25\ cm = 9.84\ inches$

11) $11\ inch = 27.94\ cm$

12) $80\ inch = 2.03\ m$

Distance Measurement

1) $10\ mi = 17,600\ yd$

2) $9\ mi = 15,840\ yd$

3) $12\ mi = 21,120\ yd$

4) $10\ mi = 52,800\ ft$

5) $15\ mi = 79,200\ ft$

6) $20\ mi = 35,200\ yd$

7) $16\ mi = 28,160\ yd$

8) $21\ mi = 110,880\ ft$

9) $6\ mi = 31,680\ ft$

10) $3\ mi = 5,280\ yd$

11) $72\ mi = 380,160\ ft$

12) $41\ mi = 72,160\ yd$

Weight Measurement

1) $0.01\ kg = 10\ g$

2) $0.2\ kg = 200\ g$

3) $0.04\ kg = 40\ g$

4) $0.05\ kg = 50\ g$

5) $0.5\ kg = 500\ g$

6) $3.2\ kg = 3,200\ g$

7) $20,000\ g = 20\ kg$

8) $3,000\ g = 3\ kg$

9) $100,000\ g = 100\ kg$

10) $150,000\ g = 150\ kg$

11) $120,000\ g = 120\ kg$

12) $200,000\ g = 200\ kg$

Day 29: Time to Test

Before You Start

- You'll need a pencil, a timer, and a four-function calculator to take the test.

- Use the answer sheet provided to record your answers. (You can cut it out or photocopy it)

- You will receive 1 point for every correct answer. There is no penalty for wrong answers.

- For each question there are four possible answers. Choose which one is best.

- It's okay to guess. You won't lose any points if you're wrong. So, make sure to answer every question before time is called, even if you have to guess on some questions.

- After you've finished the test, review the answer key to see where you went wrong and what areas you need to improve.

Good luck!

ATI TEAS 6 Math

Practice Test

2021

Total number of questions: 36

Total time: 54 Minutes

You may use a calculator on this part.

ATI TEAS 6 Mathematics Practice Test Answer Sheet

Remove (or photocopy) this answer sheet and use it to complete the practice test.

ATI TEAS 6 Mathematics Practice Test Answer Sheet		
1 Ⓐ Ⓑ Ⓒ Ⓓ	13 Ⓐ Ⓑ Ⓒ Ⓓ	25 Ⓐ Ⓑ Ⓒ Ⓓ
2 Ⓐ Ⓑ Ⓒ Ⓓ	14 Ⓐ Ⓑ Ⓒ Ⓓ	26 Ⓐ Ⓑ Ⓒ Ⓓ
3 Ⓐ Ⓑ Ⓒ Ⓓ	15 Ⓐ Ⓑ Ⓒ Ⓓ	27 Ⓐ Ⓑ Ⓒ Ⓓ
4 Ⓐ Ⓑ Ⓒ Ⓓ	16 Ⓐ Ⓑ Ⓒ Ⓓ	28 Ⓐ Ⓑ Ⓒ Ⓓ
5 Ⓐ Ⓑ Ⓒ Ⓓ	17 Ⓐ Ⓑ Ⓒ Ⓓ	29 Ⓐ Ⓑ Ⓒ Ⓓ
6 Ⓐ Ⓑ Ⓒ Ⓓ	18 Ⓐ Ⓑ Ⓒ Ⓓ	30 Ⓐ Ⓑ Ⓒ Ⓓ
7 Ⓐ Ⓑ Ⓒ Ⓓ	19 Ⓐ Ⓑ Ⓒ Ⓓ	31 Ⓐ Ⓑ Ⓒ Ⓓ
8 Ⓐ Ⓑ Ⓒ Ⓓ	20 Ⓐ Ⓑ Ⓒ Ⓓ	32 Ⓐ Ⓑ Ⓒ Ⓓ
9 Ⓐ Ⓑ Ⓒ Ⓓ	21 Ⓐ Ⓑ Ⓒ Ⓓ	33 Ⓐ Ⓑ Ⓒ Ⓓ
10 Ⓐ Ⓑ Ⓒ Ⓓ	22 Ⓐ Ⓑ Ⓒ Ⓓ	34 Ⓐ Ⓑ Ⓒ Ⓓ
11 Ⓐ Ⓑ Ⓒ Ⓓ	23 Ⓐ Ⓑ Ⓒ Ⓓ	35 Ⓐ Ⓑ Ⓒ Ⓓ
12 Ⓐ Ⓑ Ⓒ Ⓓ	24 Ⓐ Ⓑ Ⓒ Ⓓ	36 Ⓐ Ⓑ Ⓒ Ⓓ

1) If $3x - 5 = 8.5$, what is the value of $6x + 3$?

   ☐A. 13   ☐B. 15.5

   ☐C. 20.5   ☐D. 30

2) What is the area of an isosceles right triangle that has one leg that measures 8 cm?

   ☐A. 6 cm^2 ☐B. 12 cm^2

   ☐C. 18 cm^2 ☐D. 32 cm^2

3) A shirt costing \$600 is discounted 25%. After a month, the shirt is discounted another 15%. Which of the following expressions can be used to find the selling price of the shirt?

   ☐A. $(600)(0.60)$ ☐B. $(600) - 600\,(0.40)$

   ☐C. $(600)(0.25) - (200)(0.15)$ ☐D. $(600)(0.75)(0.85)$

4) Which of the following points lies on the line with equation $3x + 5y = 11$?

   ☐A. $(2, 1)$ ☐B. $(-1, 2)$

   ☐C. $(-2, 2)$ ☐D. $(2, 2)$

5) The average of five consecutive numbers is 40. What is the smallest number?

   ☐A. 38   ☐B. 36

   ☐C. 34   ☐D. 12

6) How many tiles of 8 cm^2 is needed to cover a floor of dimension 7 cm by 24 cm?

   ☐A. 6   ☐B. 12

   ☐C. 21   ☐D. 24

7) A rope weighs 600 grams per meter of length. What is the weight in kilograms of 15.2 meters of this rope? ($1\ kilograms = 1,000\ grams$)

☐A. 0.0912   ☐B. 0.912

☐C. 9.12   ☐D. 91.20

8) A chemical solution contains 6% alcohol. If there is $24\ ml$ of alcohol, what is the volume of the solution?

☐A. $240\ ml$ ☐B. $400\ ml$

☐C. $600\ ml$ ☐D. $1,200\ ml$

9) The average weight of 18 girls in a class is $60\ kg$ and the average weight of 32 boys in the same class is $62\ kg$. What is the average weight of all the 50 students in that class?

☐A. 60   ☐B. 61.28

☐C. 61.68   ☐D. 62.90

10) The price of a laptop is decreased by 10% to $360. What is its original price?

☐A. $320   ☐B. $380

☐C. $400   ☐D. $450

11) What is the median of these numbers? $4, 9, 13, 8, 15, 18, 5$

☐A. 8   ☐B. 9

☐C. 13   ☐D. 15

12) In 1999, the average worker's income increased $2,000 per year starting from $27,000 annual salary. Which equation represents income greater than average? (I = income, x = number of years after 1999)

☐A. $I > 2,000\ x + 27,000$ ☐B. $I > -2,000\ x + 27,000$

☐C. $I < -2,000\ x + 27,000$ ☐D. $I < 2,000\ x - 27,000$

13) What is the value of y in the following system of equation?

$$3x - 4y = -20$$

$$-x + 2y = 10$$

☐A. 2   ☐B. 4

☐C. 5   ☐D. 8

14) What is the area of a square whose diagonal is 6 meters?

☐ A. $20\ m^2$ ☐ B. $18\ m^2$

☐C. $12\ m^2$ ☐D. $10\ m^2$

15) The width of a box is one third of its length. The height of the box is half of its width. If the length of the box is 24 cm, what is the volume of the box?

☐A. $81\ cm^3$ ☐ B. $162\ cm^3$

☐C. $243\ cm^3$ ☐ D. $768\ cm^3$

16) If 60% of A is 20% of B, then B is what percent of A?

☐A. 3%   ☐B. 30%

☐ C. 200%   ☐D. 300%

17) A bank is offering 2.5% simple interest on a savings account. If you deposit $8,000, how much interest will you earn in five years?

☐A. $360   ☐B. $720

☐C. $1,000   ☐D. $3,600

18) 15 is What percent of 20?

☐A. 20%   ☐B. 75%

☐C. 125%   ☐D. 150%

19) In five successive hours, a car travels $40 \ km$, $45 \ km$, $50 \ km$, $35 \ km$ and $55 \ km$. In the next five hours, it travels with an average speed of $45 \ km \ per \ hour$. Find the total distance the car traveled in 10 hours.

☐A. $425 \ km$ ☐B. $450 \ km$

☐C. $475 \ km$ ☐D.$500 \ km$

20) How long does a $420- miles$ trip take moving at $60 \ miles \ per \ hour \ (mph)$?

☐A. 4 hours   ☐B. 7 hours

☐C. 7 hours and 24 minutes   ☐D. 8 hours and 10 minutes

21) Which of the following points lies on the line $4x + 6y = 20$?

☐A. $(2, 1)$ ☐B. $(-1, 3)$

☐C. $(-2, 2)$ ☐D. $(2, 2)$

22) Two third of 15 is equal to $\dfrac{2}{5}$ of what number?

☐A. 12   ☐B. 20

☐C. 25   ☐D. 60

23) The marked price of a computer is D dollar. Its price decreased by 20% in January and later increased by 15% in February. What is the final price of the computer in D dollar?

☐A. $0.80 \ D$ ☐B. $0.88 \ D$

☐C. $0.92 \ D$ ☐D. 1.20

24) A $45 shirt now selling for $28 is discounted by about what percent?

☐A. 20%   ☐B. 37.7%

☐C. 40%   ☐D. 60%

25) How many meters is 27,356 centimeters?

☐ A. $27.356 \ m$ ☐ B. $273.5600 \ m$

☐ C. $2.735600 \ m$ ☐ D. $2,735.600 \ m$

26) The score of Emma was half as that of Ava and the score of Mia was twice that of Ava. If the score of Mia was 60, what is the score of Emma?

☐A. 12   ☐B. 15

☐C. 20   ☐D. 30

A bag contains 21 balls: two green, six black, eight blue, two brown, two red and one white. If 20 balls are removed from the bag at random, what is the probability that a white ball has been removed?

☐A. $\frac{1}{9}$ ☐B. $\frac{1}{6}$

☐C. $\frac{4}{5}$ ☐D. $\frac{20}{21}$

27) A taxi driver earns $8 per 1-hour work. If he works 10 hours a day and in 1 hour he uses 2-liters petrol with price $1 for 1-liter. How much money does he earn in one day?

☐A. $90   ☐B. $88

☐C. $70   ☐D. $60

28) The price of a sofa is decreased by 15% to $476. What was its original price?

☐A. $480   ☐B. $520

☐C. $560   ☐D. $600

29) When a number is subtracted from 28 and the difference is divided by that number, the result is 3. What is the value of the number?

☐A. 2   ☐B. 4

☐C. 7   ☐D. 12

30) An angle is equal to one fourth of its supplement. What is the measure of that angle?

☐A. 18   ☐B. 24

☐ C. 36   ☐D. 45

31) John traveled 150 km in 6 hours and Alice traveled 160 km in 4 hours. What is the ratio of the average speed of John to average speed of Alice?

☐A. 3 : 2   ☐B. 2 : 3

☐C. 5 : 8   ☐D. 5 : 6

32) Right triangle ABC has two legs of lengths 5 cm (AB) and 12 cm (AC). What is the length of the third side (BC)?

☐ A. 6 cm ☐ B. 8 cm

☐ C. 13 cm ☐ D. 15 cm

33) If 75% of a class are girls, and $\frac{1}{3}$ of girls take drawing class this semester, what percent of the class are girls who take drawing class this semester?

☐A. 25%   ☐B. 28%

☐C. 35%   ☐D. 37.5%

34) From last year, the price of a table has increased from $125.00 to $185.00. The new price is what percent of the original price?

☐A. 72%   ☐B. 120%

☐C. 148%   ☐D. 160%

35) A boat sails 80 miles south and then 150 miles east. How far is the boat from its start point?

☐A. 160 miles   ☐B. 170 miles

☐C. 200 miles   ☐D. 230 miles

End of ATI TEAS 6 Mathematics Practice Test 5

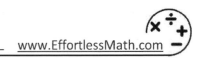

ATI TEAS 6 Math Practice Test Answers and Explanations

Now, it's time to review your results to see where you went wrong and what areas you need to improve!

TEAS 6 Math Practice Test Answer Key			
1	D	21	D
2	D	22	C
3	D	23	C
4	A	24	B
5	A	25	B
6	C	26	B
7	C	27	D
8	B	28	D
9	B	29	C
10	C	30	C
11	B	31	C
12	A	32	C
13	C	33	C
14	B	34	A
15	D	35	C
16	D	36	B
17	C		
18	B		
19	B		
20	B		

ATI TEAS 6 Mathematics Practice Test

Answers and Explanations

1) Choice D is correct

$3x - 5 = 8.5 \rightarrow 3x = 8.5 + 5 = 13.5 \rightarrow x = \frac{13.5}{3} = 4.5$

Then; $6x + 3 = 6\ (4.5) + 3 = 27 + 3 = 30$

2) Choice D is correct

First draw an isosceles triangle. Remember that two sides of the triangle are equal.

Let put a for the legs. Then:

Isosceles right triangle

$a = 8 \Rightarrow$ area of the triangle is $= \frac{1}{2}(8 \times 8) = \frac{64}{2} = 32\ cm^2$

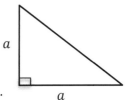

3) Choice D is correct

To find the discount, multiply the number by $(100\% - \ rate\ of\ discount)$.

Therefore, for the first discount we get: $(600)\ (100\% - 25\%) = (600)\ (0.75)$

For the next 15% discount: $(600)(0.75)(0.85)$

4) Choice A is correct

Plug in each pair of numbers in the equation: $3x + 5y = 11$

   A. $(2, 1)$: $3\ (2)\ +\ 5\ (1) = 11$
   B. $(-1, 2)$: $3\ (-1) +\ 5\ (2)\ = 7$
   C. $(-2, 2)$: $3\ (-2) +\ 5\ (2)\ = 4$
   D. $(2, 2)$: $3\ (2) + 5\ (2)\ = 16$

Choice A is correct.

5) Choice A is correct

Let x be the smallest number. Then, these are the numbers: $x, x + 1, x + 2, x + 3, x + 4$

$$average\ =\ \frac{sum\ of\ terms}{number\ of\ terms} \Rightarrow\ 40\ =\ \frac{x + (x + 1) + (x + 2) + (x + 3) + (x + 4)}{5} \Rightarrow 40$$

$$=\ \frac{5x + 10}{5} \Rightarrow\ 200\ = 5x + 10 \Rightarrow 190 = 5x \Rightarrow x = 38$$

6) Choice C is correct

The area of the floor is: $7\ cm \times 24\ cm = 168\ cm^2$, The number of tiles needed $=$

$$168 \div 8 = 21$$

7) Choice C is correct

The weight of 15.2 meters of this rope is: $15.2 \times 600\ g = 9,120\ g$, $1\ kg = 1,000\ g$, therefore, $7,320\ g \div 1,000 = 9.12\ kg$

8) Choice B is correct

6% of the volume of the solution is alcohol. Let x be the volume of the solution.

Then: $6\%\ of\ x = 24\ ml \Rightarrow 0.06\ x = 24 \Rightarrow x = 24 \div 0.06 = 400$

9) Choice B is correct

$$average = \frac{sum\ of\ terms}{number\ of\ terms}$$

The sum of the weight of all girls is: $18 \times 60 = 1,080\ kg$, The sum of the weight of all boys is: $32 \times 62 = 1,984\ kg$, The sum of the weight of all students is: $1,080 + 1,984 = 3,064\ kg$

$$average = \frac{3,064}{50} = 61.28$$

10) Choice C is correct

Let x be the original price. If the price of a laptop is decreased by 10% to $360, then:

$$90\%\ of\ x = 360 \Rightarrow 0.90x = 360 \Rightarrow x = 360 \div 0.90 = 400$$

11) Choice B is correct

Write the numbers in order: $4, 5, 8, 9, 13, 15, 18$

Since we have 7 numbers (7 is odd), then the median is the number in the middle, which is 9.

12) Choice A is correct

Let x be the number of years. Therefore, $2,000 per year equals $2,000x$. starting from $27,000 annual salary means you should add that amount to $2,000x$.

Income more than that is: $I > 2,000x + 27,000$

13) Choice C is correct

Solving Systems of Equations by Elimination

$3x - 4y = -20$
$-x + 2y = 10$ Multiply the second equation by 3, then add it to the first equation.

$$\begin{matrix} 3x - 4y = -20 \\ 3(-x + 2y = 10) \end{matrix} \Rightarrow \begin{matrix} 3x - 4y = -20 \\ -3x + 6y = 30) \end{matrix} \Rightarrow 2y = 10 \Rightarrow y = 5$$

14) Choice B is correct

The diagonal of the square is 6 meters. Let x be the side.

Use Pythagorean Theorem: $a^2 + b^2 = c^2$

$x^2 + x^2 = 6^2 \Rightarrow 2x^2 = 6^2 \Rightarrow 2x^2 = 36 \Rightarrow x^2 = 18 \Rightarrow x = \sqrt{18}$

The area of the square is: $\sqrt{18} \times \sqrt{18} = 18 \ m^2$

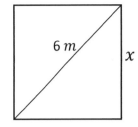

15) Choice D is correct

If the length of the box is 24, then the width of the box is one third of it, 8, and the height of the box is 4 (half of the width). The volume of the box is: $V = lwh = (24)(8)(4) = 768$

16) Choice D is correct

Write the equation and solve for B: $0.60A = 0.20B$, divide both sides by 0.20, then:

$\frac{0.60}{0.20} A = B$, therefore: $B = 3A$, and B is 3 times of A or it's 300% of A.

17) Choice C is correct

Use simple interest formula: $I = prt$ ($I = interest, \ p = principal, \ r = rate, \ t = time$)

$I = (8,000)(0.025)(5) = 1,000$

18) Choice B is correct

Use percent formula: $part = \frac{percent}{100} \times whole$. $15 = \frac{percent}{100} \times 20 \Rightarrow 15 = \frac{percent \times 20}{100} \Rightarrow$

$15 = \frac{percent \times 2}{10}$, multiply both sides by 10. $150 = percent \times 2$, divide both sides by 2.

$75 = percent$

19) Choice B is correct

Add the first 5 numbers. $40 + 45 + 50 + 35 + 55 = 225$

To find the distance traveled in the next 5 hours, multiply the average by number of hours.

Distance = Average × Rate = $45 \times 5 = 225$,   Add both numbers. $225 + 225 = 450$

20) Choice B is correct

Use distance formula: $Distance = Rate \times time \Rightarrow 420 = 60 \times T$, divide both sides by 60.

$\frac{420}{60} = T \Rightarrow T = 7$ hours

21) Choice D is correct.

Plug in each pair of numbers in the equation. The answer should be 20.

A. $(2, 1)$: $4(2) + 6(1) = 14$ No!

B. $(-1, 3)$: $4(-1) + 6(2) = 8$ No!

C. $(-2, 2)$: $4(-2) + 6(2) = 4$ No!

D. $(2, 2)$: $4(2) + 6(2) = 20$ Yes!

22) Choice C is correct

Let x be the number. Write the equation and solve for x.

$\frac{2}{3} \times 15 = \frac{2}{5} \cdot x \Rightarrow \frac{2 \times 15}{3} = \frac{2x}{5}$, use cross multiplication to solve for x. $5 \times 30 = 2x \times 3 \Rightarrow$

$$150 = 6x \Rightarrow x = 25$$

23) Choice C is correct

To find the discount, multiply the number by $(100\% - rate\ of\ discount)$.

Therefore, for the first discount we get: $(D)(100\% - 20\%) = (D)(0.80) = 0.80\ D$

For increase of 15%: $(0.80D)(100\% + 15\%) = (0.80\ D)(1.15) = 0.92\ D = 92\%\ of\ D$

24) Choice B is correct

Use the formula for Percent of Change: $\frac{New\ Value - Old\ Value}{Old\ Value} \times 100\%$

$\frac{28-45}{45} \times 100\% = -37.7\%$ (negative sign here means that the new price is less than old price).

25) Choice B is correct

1 meter $=$ 100 centimeters. Then: $27,356 \times 0.01 = 273.56$

26) Choice B is correct

If the score of Mia was 60, therefore the score of Ava is 30. Since, the score of Emma was half as that of Ava, therefore, the score of Emma is 15.

27) Choice D is correct

If 20 balls are removed from the bag at random, there will be one ball in the bag. The probability of choosing a white ball is 1 out of 21. Therefore, the probability of not choosing a white ball is 20 out of 21 and the probability of having not a white ball after removing 20 balls is the same.

28) Choice D is correct

$\$8 \times 10 = \$80$,   Petrol use: $10 \times 2 = 20$ liters,   Petrol cost: $20 \times \$1 = \$20$

Money earned: $\$80 - \$20 = \$60$

29) Choice C is correct

Let x be the original price. If the price of the sofa is decreased by 15% to \$476, then: $85\%\ of\ x = 476 \Rightarrow 0.85x = 476 \Rightarrow x = 476 \div 0.85 = 560$

30) Choice C is correct

Let x be the number. Write the equation and solve for x. $(28 - x) \div x = 3$

Multiply both sides by x. $(28 - x) = 3x$, then add x both sides. $28 = 4x$, now divide both sides by 4. $x = 7$

31) Choice C is correct

The sum of supplement angles is 180. Let x be that angle. Therefore, $x + 4x = 180$

$5x = 180$, divide both sides by 5: $x = 36$

32) Choice C is correct

The average speed of John is: $150 \div 6 = 25 \ km$. The average speed of Alice is:

$160 \div 4 = 40 \ km$. Write the ratio and simplify. $25 : 40 \ \Rightarrow \ 5 : 8$

33) Choice C is correct

Use Pythagorean Theorem: $a^2 + b^2 = c^2$

$5^2 + 12^2 = c^2 \ \Rightarrow \ 25 + 144 = c^2 \ \Rightarrow \ 169 = c^2 \Rightarrow c = 13$

34) Choice A is correct

The percent of girls take drawing class is: $75\% \times \frac{1}{3} = 25\%$

35) Choice C is correct

The question is this: 185.00 is what percent of 125.00? Use percent formula:

$\frac{185}{125} = 1.48$ or 148%

36) Choice B is correct

Use the information provided in the question to draw the shape.

Use Pythagorean Theorem: $a^2 + b^2 = c^2$

$80^2 + 150^2 = c^2 \Rightarrow 6,400 + 22,500 = c^2 \Rightarrow 28,900 = c^2 \Rightarrow c = 170$

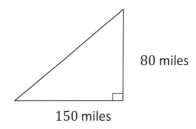

80 miles

150 miles

Day 30: A Realistic ATI TEAS 6 Math Test

Time to experience a REAL ATI TEAS 6 Math Test

Take the following practice ATI TEAS 6 Math Test to simulate the test day experience. After you've finished, score your test using the answer key.

Before You Start

- You'll need a pencil, a timer, and a four-function calculator to take the test.

- After you've finished the test, review the answer key to see where you went wrong.

- You will receive 1 point for every correct answer. There is no penalty for wrong answers.

- **Keep Strict Timing on the Test Section!**

Good Luck!

Mathematics is not only real, but it is the only reality. ~ Martin Gardner

ATI TEAS 6 Math

Practice Test

2021

Total number of questions: 36

Total time: 54 Minutes

You may use a calculator on this part.

ATI TEAS 6 Mathematics Practice Test Answer Sheet

Remove (or photocopy) this answer sheet and use it to complete the practice test.

ATI TEAS 6 Mathematics Practice Test Answer Sheet		
1 Ⓐ Ⓑ Ⓒ Ⓓ	13 Ⓐ Ⓑ Ⓒ Ⓓ	25 Ⓐ Ⓑ Ⓒ Ⓓ
2 Ⓐ Ⓑ Ⓒ Ⓓ	14 Ⓐ Ⓑ Ⓒ Ⓓ	26 Ⓐ Ⓑ Ⓒ Ⓓ
3 Ⓐ Ⓑ Ⓒ Ⓓ	15 Ⓐ Ⓑ Ⓒ Ⓓ	27 Ⓐ Ⓑ Ⓒ Ⓓ
4 Ⓐ Ⓑ Ⓒ Ⓓ	16 Ⓐ Ⓑ Ⓒ Ⓓ	28 Ⓐ Ⓑ Ⓒ Ⓓ
5 Ⓐ Ⓑ Ⓒ Ⓓ	17 Ⓐ Ⓑ Ⓒ Ⓓ	29 Ⓐ Ⓑ Ⓒ Ⓓ
6 Ⓐ Ⓑ Ⓒ Ⓓ	18 Ⓐ Ⓑ Ⓒ Ⓓ	30 Ⓐ Ⓑ Ⓒ Ⓓ
7 Ⓐ Ⓑ Ⓒ Ⓓ	19 Ⓐ Ⓑ Ⓒ Ⓓ	31 Ⓐ Ⓑ Ⓒ Ⓓ
8 Ⓐ Ⓑ Ⓒ Ⓓ	20 Ⓐ Ⓑ Ⓒ Ⓓ	32 Ⓐ Ⓑ Ⓒ Ⓓ
9 Ⓐ Ⓑ Ⓒ Ⓓ	21 Ⓐ Ⓑ Ⓒ Ⓓ	33 Ⓐ Ⓑ Ⓒ Ⓓ
10 Ⓐ Ⓑ Ⓒ Ⓓ	22 Ⓐ Ⓑ Ⓒ Ⓓ	34 Ⓐ Ⓑ Ⓒ Ⓓ
11 Ⓐ Ⓑ Ⓒ Ⓓ	23 Ⓐ Ⓑ Ⓒ Ⓓ	35 Ⓐ Ⓑ Ⓒ Ⓓ
12 Ⓐ Ⓑ Ⓒ Ⓓ	24 Ⓐ Ⓑ Ⓒ Ⓓ	36 Ⓐ Ⓑ Ⓒ Ⓓ

1) The sum of two numbers is x. If one of the numbers is 9, then two times the other number would be?

☐A. $2x$ ☐B. $2 + x \times 2$

☐C. $2(x + 9)$ ☐D. $2(x - 9)$

2) A tree 32 feet tall casts a shadow 12 feet long. Jack is 6 feet tall. How long is Jack's shadow?

☐A. $2.25\ ft$ ☐B. $4\ ft$

☐C. $4.25\ ft$ ☐D. $8\ ft$

3) What is the product of all possible values of x in the following equation?

$$|2x - 6| = 12$$

☐A. -27 ☐B. -3

☐C. 9 ☐D. 27

4) What is the slope of a line that is perpendicular to the line $3x - y = 6$?

☐A. -3 ☐B. $-\frac{1}{3}$

☐C. 2 ☐D. 6

5) What is the value of the expression $3(x - 2y) + (2 - x)^2$ when $x = 5$ and $y = -3$?

☐A. -22 ☐B. 24

☐C. 42 ☐D. 88

6) $\dfrac{(15\ feet + 7\ yards)}{4} = $ _____

☐A. $4\ ft$ ☐B. $7\ ft$

☐C. $9\ ft$ ☐D. $28\ ft$

7) Which of the following answers represents the compound inequality $-4 \leq 4x - 8 < 16$?

   ☐A. $-2 \leq x \leq 8$ ☐C. $1 < x \leq 6$

   ☐B. $-2 < x \leq 8$ ☐D. $1 \leq x < 6$

8) What is the volume of a box with the following dimensions?

   Hight = 4 cm Width = 5 cm Length = 6 cm

   ☐A. 15 cm^3 ☐B. 60 cm^3

   ☐C. 90 cm^3 ☐D. 120 cm^3

9) Simplify the expression.

$$(6x^3 - 8x^2 + 2x^4) - (4x^2 - 2x^4 + 2x^3)$$

   ☐A. $4x^4 + 4x^3 - 12x^2$ ☐B. $4x^3 - 12x^2$

   ☐C. $4x^4 + 4x^3 + 12x^2$ ☐D. $8x^3 - 12x^2$

10) In two successive years, the population of a town is increased by 15% and 20%. What percent of the population is increased after two years?

   ☐A. 32%   ☐B. 35%

   ☐C. 38%   ☐D. 68%

11) Last week 24,000 fans attended a football match. This week three times as many bought tickets, but one sixth of them cancelled their tickets. How many are attending this week?

   ☐A. 48,000   ☐B. 54,000

   ☐C. 60,000   ☐D. 72,000

12) $\frac{7}{25}$ is equals to:

   ☐A. 0.3   ☐B. 2.8

   ☐C. 0.03   ☐D. 0.28

13) In the simplest form, $\frac{18}{24}$ is

   ☐A. $\frac{2}{3}$ ☐B. $\frac{3}{2}$

   ☐C. $\frac{4}{3}$ ☐D. $\frac{3}{4}$

14) The mean of 50 test scores was calculated as 88. But, it turned out that one of the scores was misread as 94 but it was 69. What is the correct mean of the test scores?

   ☐A. 85   ☐B. 87

   ☐C. 87.5   ☐D. 88.5

15) If two angles in a triangle measure 53 degrees and 45 degrees, what is the value of the third angle?

   ☐A. 8 degrees   ☐B. 42 degrees

   ☐C. 82 degrees   ☐D. 98 degrees

16) What is the area of a square whose diagonal is 8?

   ☐A. 16   ☐B. 32

   ☐C. 36   ☐D. 64

17) Anita's trick–or–treat bag contains 12 pieces of chocolate, 18 suckers, 18 pieces of gum, 24 pieces of licorice. If she randomly pulls a piece of candy from her bag, what is the probability of her pulling out a piece of sucker?

   ☐A. $\frac{1}{3}$ ☐B. $\frac{1}{4}$

   ☐C. $\frac{1}{6}$ ☐D. $\frac{1}{12}$

18) The perimeter of a rectangular yard is 60 meters. What is its length if its width is twice its length?

☐A. 10 meters   ☐B. 18 meters

☐C. 20 meters   ☐D. 24 meters

19) The average of 6 numbers is 12. The average of 4 of those numbers is 10. What is the average of the other two numbers?

☐A. 10   ☐B. 12

☐C. 14   ☐D. 16

20) What is the value of x in the following system of equations?

$$2x + 5y = 11$$
$$4x - 2y = -14$$

☐A. −1   ☐B. 1

☐C. −2   ☐D. 4

21) The perimeter of the trapezoid below is 36 cm. What is its area?

☐A. 576 cm^2 ☐B. 70 cm^2

☐C. 48 cm^2 ☐D. 24 cm^2

22) A card is drawn at random from a standard 52–card deck, what is the probability that the card is of Hearts? (The deck includes 13 of each suit clubs, diamonds, hearts, and spades)

☐A. $\dfrac{1}{3}$ ☐B. $\dfrac{1}{4}$

☐C. $\dfrac{1}{6}$ ☐D. $\dfrac{1}{52}$

23) The ratio of boys and girls in a class is $4:7$. If there are 44 students in the class, how many more boys should be enrolled to make the ratio $1:1$?

    ☐A. 8   ☐B. 10

    ☐C. 12   ☐D. 14

24) Mr. Jones saves $2,500 out of his monthly family income of $55,000. What fractional part of his income does he save?

    ☐A. $\frac{1}{22}$ ☐B. $\frac{1}{11}$

    ☐C. $\frac{3}{25}$ ☐D. $\frac{2}{15}$

25) What is the value of x in the following equation? $\frac{2}{3}x + \frac{1}{6} = \frac{1}{3}$

    ☐A. 6   ☐B. $\frac{1}{2}$

    ☐C. $\frac{1}{3}$ ☐D. $\frac{1}{4}$

26) A bank is offering 3.5% simple interest on a savings account. If you deposit $12,000, how much interest will you earn in two years?

    ☐A. $420   ☐B. $840

    ☐C. $4,200   ☐D. $8,400

27) Simplify $6x^2y^3(2x^2y)^3 =$

    ☐A. $12x^4y^6$ ☐B. $12x^8y^6$

    ☐C. $48x^4y^6$ ☐D. $48x^8y^6$

28) What is the surface area of the cylinder below?

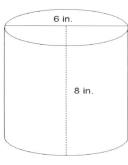

□A. $48\,\pi\,in^2$ □B. $57\,\pi\,in^2$

□C. $66\,\pi\,in^2$ □D. $288\,\pi\,in^2$

29) What is the median of these numbers? $2, 27, 28, 19, 67, 44, 35$

□A. 19   □B. 28

□C. 44   □D. 35

30) What is the equivalent temperature of $104°F$ in Celsius? $C = \dfrac{5}{9}(F - 32)$

□A. 32   □B. 40

□C. 48   □D. 52

31) If 40% of a number is 4, what is the number?

□A. 4   □B. 8

□C. 10   □D. 12

32) The circle graph below shows all Mr. Green's expenses for last month. If he spent $660 on his car, how much did he spend for his rent?

Mr. Green's monthly expenses

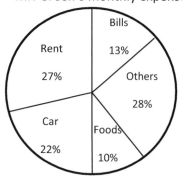

□A. $700   □B. $740

□C. $780   □D. $810

33) Jason is 9 miles ahead of Joe running at 5.5 miles per hour and Joe is running at the speed of 7 miles per hour. How long does it take Joe to catch Jason?

☐A. 3 hours   ☐B. 4 hours

☐C. 6 hours   ☐D. 8 hours

34) 55 students took an exam and 11 of them failed. What percent of the students passed the exam?

☐A. 20%   ☐B. 40%

☐C. 60%   ☐D. 80%

35) If 150% of a number is 75, then what is the 90% of that number?

☐A. 45   ☐B. 50

☐C. 70   ☐D.85

36) Julie gives 8 pieces of candy to each of her friends. If Julie gives all her candy away, which amount of candy could have been the amount she distributed?

☐A. 187   ☐B. 216

☐C. 223   ☐D.243

End of ATI TEAS 6 Mathematics Practice Test

ATI TEAS 6 Math Practice Test Answers and Explanations

Now, it's time to review your results to see where you went wrong and what areas you need to improve!

TEAS 6 Math Practice Test Answer Key			
1	D	21	B
2	A	22	B
3	A	23	C
4	B	24	A
5	C	25	D
6	C	26	B
7	D	27	D
8	D	28	C
9	A	29	B
10	C	30	B
11	C	31	C
12	D	32	D
13	D	33	C
14	C	34	D
15	C	35	A
16	B	36	B
17	B		
18	A		
19	D		
20	C		

ATI TEAS 6 Mathematics Practice Test
Answers and Explanations

1) Choice D is correct

Let a and b be the numbers. Then: $a + b = x$. $a = 9 \rightarrow 9 + b = x \rightarrow b = x - 9$

$2b = 2(x - 9)$

2) Choice A is correct

Write a proportion and solve for the missing number. $\frac{32}{12} = \frac{6}{x} \rightarrow 32x = 6 \times 12 = 72$

$32x = 72 \rightarrow x = \dfrac{72}{32} = 2.25$

3) Choice A is correct

To solve absolute values equations, write two equations. $2x - 6$ can equal positive 12, or negative 12. Therefore, $2x - 6 = 12 \Rightarrow 2x = 18 \Rightarrow x = 9$.

$2x - 6 = -12 \Rightarrow 2x = -12 + 6 = -6 \Rightarrow x = -3$.

Find the product of solutions: $-3 \times 9 = -27$

4) Choice B is correct

The equation of a line in slope intercept form is: $y = mx + b$. Solve for y. $3x - y = 6 \rightarrow$

$-y = -3x + 6$. Divide both sides by (-1). Then: $-y = -3x + 6 \rightarrow y = 3x - 6$

The slope of this line is 3. The product of the slopes of two perpendicular lines is -1. Therefore, the slope of a line that is perpendicular to this line is:

$$m_1 \times m_2 = -1 \Rightarrow 3 \times m_2 = -1 \Rightarrow m_2 = \frac{-1}{3} = -\frac{1}{3}$$

5) Choice C is correct

Plug in the value of x and y. $3(x - 2y) + (2 - x)^2$ when $x = 5$ and $y = -3$

$3(x - 2y) + (2 - x)^2 = 3(5 - 2(-3)) + (2 - 5)^2 = 3(5 + 6) + (-3)^2 = 33 + 9 = 42$

6) Choice C is correct

$$1 \ yard = 12 \ feet$$

$$\frac{(15 \ feet \ + \ 7 \ yards)}{4} = \frac{(15 \ feet \ + \ 21 \ feet)}{4} = \frac{(36 \ feet \ )}{4} = 9 \ feet$$

7) Choice D is correct

Solve for x. $x - 4 \leq 4x - 8 < 16 \Rightarrow$ (add 8 all sides) $-4 + 8 < 4x - 8 + 8 < 16 + 8 \Rightarrow$

$4 < 4x < 24 \Rightarrow$ (divide all sides by 4) $1 \leq x < 6$

x is between 1 and 6. Choice D represents this inequality.

8) Choice D is correct

$Volume\ of\ a\ box\ =\ length\ \times\ width\ \times\ height\ =\ 4 \times 5 \times 6 = 120$

9) Choice A is correct

Simplify and combine like terms. $(6x^3 - 8x^2 + 2x^4) - (4x^2 - 2x^4 + 2x^3) \Rightarrow$
$(6x^3 - 8x^2 + 2x^4) - 4x^2 + 2x^4 - 2x^3 \Rightarrow 4x^4 + 4x^3 - 12x^2$

10) Choice C is correct

the population is increased by 15% and 20%. 15% increase changes the population to 115% of original population. For the second increase, multiply the result by 120%.

$(1.15) \times (1.20) = 1.38 = 138\%$. 38 percent of the population is increased after two years.

11) Choice C is correct

Three times of 24,000 is 72,000. One sixth of them cancelled their tickets.

One sixth of 72,000 equals 12,000 ($\frac{1}{6} \times 72,000 = 12,000$).

60,000 ($72,000 - 12,000 = 60,000$) fans are attending this week

12) Choice D is correct

$\frac{7}{25} = 0.28$

13) Choice D is correct

$\frac{18}{24} = \frac{3}{4}$

14) Choice C is correct

$average\ (mean)\ =\ \frac{sum\ of\ terms}{number\ of\ terms} \Rightarrow 88 = \frac{sum\ of\ terms}{50} \Rightarrow sum = 88 \times 50 = 4,400$

The difference of 94 and 69 is 25. Therefore, 25 should be subtracted from the sum.

$4,400 - 25 = 4,375,\ mean\ \frac{sum\ of\ terms}{number\ of\ terms} \Rightarrow mean = \frac{4,375}{50} = 87.5$

15) Choice C is correct

All angles in a triangle sum up to 180 degrees. $53 + 45 = 98$. $180 - 98 = 82$,

The third angle is 82 degrees.

16) Choice B is correct

The diagonal of the square is 8. Let x be the side.

Use Pythagorean Theorem: $a^2 + b^2 = c^2$

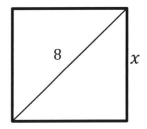

$x^2 + x^2 = 8^2 \Rightarrow 2x^2 = 8^2 \Rightarrow 2x^2 = 64 \Rightarrow x^2 = 32 \Rightarrow x = \sqrt{32}$

The area of the square is: $\sqrt{32} \times \sqrt{32} = 32$

17) Choice B is correct

$Probability = \dfrac{number\ of\ desired\ outcomes}{number\ of\ total\ outcomes} = \dfrac{18}{12 + 18 + 18 + 24} = \dfrac{18}{72} = \dfrac{1}{4}$

18) Choice A is correct

The width of the rectangle is twice its length. Let x be the length. Then, $width = 2x$

Perimeter of the rectangle is $2\ (width + length)\ = 2(2x + x) = 60 \Rightarrow 6x = 60 \Rightarrow x = 10$

Length of the rectangle is 10 meters.

19) Choice D is correct

$average = \dfrac{sum\ of\ terms}{number\ of\ terms} \Rightarrow$ (average of 6 numbers) $12 = \dfrac{sum\ of\ numbers}{6} \Rightarrow$ sum of 6 numbers is $12 \times 6 = 72$

(average of 4 numbers) $10 = \dfrac{sum\ of\ numbers}{4} \Rightarrow$ sum of 4 numbers is $10 \times 4 = 40$

$sum\ of\ 6\ numbers - sum\ of\ 4\ numbers = sum\ of\ 2\ numbers$, $72 - 40 = 32$,

average of 2 numbers $= \dfrac{32}{2} = 16$

20) Choice C is correct

Solving Systems of Equations by Elimination

Multiply the first equation by (-2), then add it to the second equation.

$\begin{array}{r} -2(2x + 5y = 11) \\ 4x - 2y = -14 \\ \hline \end{array} \Rightarrow \begin{array}{r} -4x - 10y = -22 \\ 4x - 2y = -14 \\ \hline \end{array} \Rightarrow -12y = -36 \Rightarrow y = 3$

Plug in the value of y into one of the equations and solve for x.

$2x + 5(3) = 11 \Rightarrow 2x + 15 = 11 \Rightarrow 2x = -4 \Rightarrow x = -2$

21) Choice B is correct

The perimeter of the trapezoid is $36\ cm$.

Therefore, the missing side (height) is $= 36 - 8 - 12 - 6\ = 10$

Area of a trapezoid: $A\ =\ \frac{1}{2}\ h\ (b_1\ +\ b_2) = \frac{1}{2}\ (10)\ (6\ +\ 8)\ = 70$

22) Choice B is correct

The probability of choosing a Hearts is $\frac{13}{52} = \frac{1}{4}$

23) Choice C is correct

Th ratio of boy to girls is $4:7$. Therefore, there are 4 boys out of 11 students. To find the answer, first divide the total number of students by 11, then multiply the result by 4. $44 \div 11 = 4 \Rightarrow 4 \times 4 = 16$. There are 16 boys and $28\ (44 - 16)$ girls. So, 12 more boys should be enrolled to make the ratio $1:1$

24) Choice A is correct

2,500 out of 55,000 equals to $\dfrac{2,500}{55,000} = \dfrac{25}{550} = \dfrac{1}{22}$

25) Choice D is correct

Isolate and solve for x. $\frac{2}{3}x + \frac{1}{6} = \frac{1}{3} \Rightarrow \frac{2}{3}x = \frac{1}{3} - \frac{1}{6} = \frac{1}{6} \Rightarrow \frac{2}{3}x = \frac{1}{6}$

Multiply both sides by the reciprocal of the coefficient of x. $(\frac{3}{2})\frac{2}{3}x = \frac{1}{6}(\frac{3}{2}) \Rightarrow x = \frac{3}{12} = \frac{1}{4}$

26) Choice B is correct

Use simple interest formula: $I = prt$ (I = interest, p = principal, r = rate, t = time)

$I = (12,000)(0.035)(2) = 840$

27) Choice D is correct

Simplify. $6x^2y^3(2x^2y)^3 = 6x^2y^3(8x^6y^3) = 48x^8y^6$

28) Choice C is correct

Surface Area of a cylinder $= 2\pi r\ (r + h)$, The radius of the cylinder is $3(6 \div 2)$ inches and its height is 8 inches. Therefore, Surface Area of a cylinder $= 2\pi(3)(3 + 8) = 66\ \pi$

29) Choice B is correct

Write the numbers in order: $2, 19, 27, 28, 35, 44, 67$.

Median is the number in the middle. So, the median is 28.

30) Choice B is correct

Plug in 104 for F and then solve for C. $C = \frac{5}{9}(F - 32) \Rightarrow C = \frac{5}{9}(104 - 32) \Rightarrow$

$$C = \frac{5}{9}(72) = 40$$

31) Choice C is correct

Let x be the number. Write the equation and solve for x. $40\% \ of \ x = 4 \Rightarrow 0.40 \ x = 4 \Rightarrow x = 4 \div 0.40 = 10$

32) Choice D is correct

Let x be all expenses, then $\frac{22}{100}x = \$660 \rightarrow x = \frac{100 \times \$660}{22} = \$3,000$. He spent for his rent: $\frac{27}{100} \times \$3,000 = \$810$

33) Choice C is correct

The distance between Jason and Joe is 9 miles. Jason running at 5.5 miles per hour and Joe is running at the speed of 7 miles per hour. Therefore, every hour the distance is 1.5 miles less.

$9 \div 1.5 = 6$

34) Choice D is correct

The failing rate is 11 out of $55 = \frac{11}{55}$. Change the fraction to percent: $\frac{11}{55} \times 100\% = 20\%$

20 percent of students failed. Therefore, 80 percent of students passed the exam.

35) Choice A is correct

First, find the number. Let x be the number. Write the equation and solve for x.

150% of a number is 75, then: $1.5 \times x = 75 \Rightarrow x = 75 \div 1.5 = 50$

90% of 50 is: $\qquad 0.9 \times 50 = 45$

36) Choice B is correct

Since Julie gives 8 pieces of candy to each of her friends, then, then number of pieces of candies must be divisible by 8.

   A. $187 \div 8 = 23.375$

   B. $216 \div 8 = 27$

   C. $223 \div 8 = 27.875$

D. $343 \div 8 = 42.875$

Only choice B gives a whole number.

www.EffortlessMath.com

... So Much More Online!

✓ FREE Math lessons

✓ More Math learning books!

✓ Mathematics Worksheets

✓ Online Math Tutors

Need a PDF version of this book?

Visit www.EffortlessMath.com

Receive the PDF version of this book or get another FREE book!

Thank you for using our Book!

Do you LOVE this book?

Then, you can get the PDF version of this book or another book absolutely FREE!

Please email us at:

info@EffortlessMath.com

for details.

Author's Final Note

I hope you enjoyed reading this book. You've made it through the book! Great job!

First of all, thank you for purchasing this study guide. I know you could have picked any number of books to help you prepare for your ATI TEAS 6 Math test, but you picked this book and for that I am extremely grateful.

It took me years to write this study guide for the ATI TEAS 6 Math because I wanted to prepare a comprehensive ATI TEAS 6 Math study guide to help test takers make the most effective use of their valuable time while preparing for the test.

After teaching and tutoring math for over a decade, I've gathered my personal notes and lessons to develop this study guide. It is my greatest hope that the lessons in this book could help you prepare for your test successfully.

If you have any questions, please contact me at reza@effortlessmath.com and I will be glad to assist. Your feedback will help me to greatly improve the quality of my books in the future and make this book even better. Furthermore, I expect that I have made a few minor errors somewhere in this study guide. If you think this to be the case, please let me know so I can fix the issue as soon as possible.

If you enjoyed this book and found some benefit in reading this, I'd like to hear from you and hope that you could take a quick minute to post a review on the book's Amazon page. To leave your valuable feedback, please visit: azmn.to/3baE5SK

Or scan this QR code.

I personally go over every single review, to make sure my books really are reaching out and helping students and test takers. Please help me help ATI TEAS 6 Math test takers, by leaving a review!

I wish you all the best in your future success!

Reza Nazari

Math teacher and author

Made in United States
Orlando, FL
05 May 2023

32850787R00100